Advance praise for *Raising God-First Kids*

I first met Barbara Curtis when we just delivered my ninth baby premat my baby was in the NICU. Barba rp, was in that hospital, too, recovering from a complicated knee surgery. Looking back, I see God's hand. There aren't many firsthand mentors out there for forty-something women who are still having babies. God made very sure that I knew that an extraordinary mentor was right there in my own backyard.

Everyone who knew Barbara, and certainly everyone who was familiar with her writings, knew she was an intense and passionate woman. She lived her life fully and wholeheartedly. One of Barbara's greatest gifts was her unique story. She recognized that the transformation she experienced could have only come from a mighty God. God's gift to Barbara was her story of redemption, and Barbara's gift to all of us was her willingness to share the story.

During the last year of her life, Barbara wrote a book. You hold that book in your hands. It's almost as if she knew, as if she pushed herself to get these things down on paper before she died. She passionately wanted to pass this wisdom on to you. I have the sure sense that *Raising God-First Kids in a Me-First World* will go a long way toward filling in the wisdom gaps for many of us. In the weeks since she died, I have heard astounding stories of rippling grace. Barbara Curtis's influence stretched far and wide.

We would be well served to listen to what Barbara has to say and learn from her experience. We are privileged to have the gift of this book.

—Elizabeth Foss

Barbara Curtis offers insight, inspiration, and encouragement to parents who seek to raise strong and faithful families. With characteristic wit and wisdom, *Raising God-First Kids in a Me-First World* provides plenty of personal examples from both Barbara's permissive past and her bold second take at parenting in the Church. She's a Catholic mom's mom, willing to share her experience for the benefit of parents and children so that all families can do what they are meant to do: Glorify God.

—Marybeth Hicks, author

Raising God-First Kids in a Me-First World is delightful, yet it's bitter-sweet knowing that this will be the last book of hers we'll get to have. I'm grateful for the wonderful connection Barbara has with her readers—and this reader in particular! We both have large families, we both have been blessed with having sons born with Down syndrome, and we both have experienced the incredible grace of returning to our Catholic faith. I value highly the way Barbara has shared the joys and sorrows that come from having children grow into their adult lives—and the wisdom to know how to deal with the heartache that comes when some of them choose a path different from how they were raised. Thank you, Barbara, and thank you, Curtis family, for giving many readers a useful look at the eternal importance of raising God-first kids in this me-first world.

—Martha Sears, coauthor of *The Complete Book of Christian Parenting and Child Care*

Barbara Curtis draws on her experience as both a mother of twelve and a spiritual seeker who traveled her own rocky path, and in doing so has created a book brimming with wisdom and powerful advice. Just as the title promises, modern parents will feel encouraged, empowered, and equipped to raise God-first kids in a me-first world.

—Jennifer Fulwiler, ConversionDiary.com

RAISING GOD-FIRST KIDS IN A ME-FIRST WORLD

. . .

Barbara Curtis

PUBLISHED BY FRANCISCAN MEDIA
Cincinnati, Ohio

Scripture passages have been taken from the *Revised Standard Version*, Catholic edition. Copyright 1946, 1952, 1971 by the Division of Christian Education of the National Council of Churches of Christ in the USA. Used by permission. All rights reserved.
Quotes are taken from the English translation of the *Catechism of the Catholic Church* for the United States of America (indicated as *CCC*), 2nd ed. Copyright 1997 by United States Catholic Conference—Libreria Editrice Vaticana.

Cover and book design by Mark Sullivan
Cover image © iStockphoto | René Mansi

LIBRARY OF CONGRESS CATALOGING-IN-PUBLICATION DATA
Curtis, Barbara, 1948-
Raising God first kids in a me first world / Barbara Curtis.
pages cm
Includes bibliographical references.
ISBN 978-1-61636-534-9 (alk. paper)
1. Child rearing—Religious aspects—Christianity. 2. Parenting—Religious aspects—Christianity. 3. Selfishness. I. Title.
BV4529.C865 2013
248.8'45—dc23
2012049152

ISBN 978-1-61636-534-9
Copyright © 2013, Barbara Curtis. All rights reserved.
Published by Servant Books, an imprint of Franciscan Media.
28 W. Liberty St.
Cincinnati, OH 45202
www.FranciscanMedia.org

Printed in the United States of America.
Printed on acid-free paper.
13 14 15 16 17   5 4 3 2 1

Contents

. . .

DEDICATION

Barbara wanted to dedicate this book to
mothers and fathers everywhere,
old and young alike.
You are parents for such a time as this.

FOREWORD

Barbara finished writing this book six weeks before she died, suddenly, on October 30, 2012. In that respect, this book could be said to be the culmination of her life's work. But that would be selling her legacy short. Cherished in life by me and beloved by her twelve children, their spouses, fourteen grandchildren (with two more due in 2013), treasured friends, and the countless host she touched through her writing and speaking—her life's work will continue as we live out our lives, practicing and implementing the wisdom she taught.

Barbara and I were in our fourth decade of raising teenagers when she died. With twelve children from ages twelve to forty-two (four with special needs, three of whom were adopted) and fourteen grandchildren from ages one to twenty, we've seen our share of parenting in just about every sort of circumstance…from tragedy to triumph. It hasn't always been easy or rewarding, and we certainly weren't always respected at the time. But raising our children is the most important mission God gives us as parents—and we often don't have a clue how to carry that out.

Barbara's desire for this book was to impart to her readers the reality of God's grace, wisdom, and knowledge, which comes when you invite him into your parenting. Every child born is unique and special—created by God with a purpose in mind. And he created parents to raise that child in order to fulfill that plan. With that in mind, it is our job to ask God for and constantly listen for his counsel through the Holy Spirit to help us find our child's gifts, strengths, and weaknesses in order to guide them on his path.

As you will see from our backgrounds, Barbara doesn't harp or come across as superior. Whether she was speaking or writing, one thing you could count on from Barbara was an authentic and gentle voice. The 1940s Frank Capra hit *Meet John Doe* contained a line she loved so much that she made it her own: "Say something simple and real, something with hope in it"—and her life bore that out. This book is her message of hope to you. We live in challenging times. Home is where each of our stories begins, and as Barbara would say, "We were born for times such as these."

Papa Tripp
December 2012

. . .

ACKNOWLEDGMENTS

As Barbara's husband and closest friend, I know there's a lifetime of friends, family, and fellow pilgrims that she would have wanted to thank for their contributions in her life and to the writing of this last book, which she finished six weeks before her untimely death.

Her two closest friends, Ann Stewart and Leona Choy, deserve special thanks for loving her as true friends and pilgrims. Thanks must certainly be made to her worldwide blogging family from whom she learned so much and who held her up through their love and prayers. Also, Barbara would want to thank all of her children and grandchildren, whom she loved so much, and from whom she learned firsthand how to raise children to love and serve God. A special thanks to her editor, Claudia Volkman, and Franciscan Media for having the faith to go ahead and release Barbara's last written work. Most of all though, she'd want to thank her loving Heavenly Father for the time he gave her to become what he called her to be: a loving mother who sought to raise her children and others to follow God's ways and not the world's.

Nil Sine Dominus—Nothing without Providence

Papa Tripp
December 2012

CHAPTER ONE

Parenting Roots and Wings

"Should you really be writing this book?"

That's what the Great Discourager keeps whispering in my ear, parading pictures of role-model Catholic mothers I've met—in person or on the Internet—since I came into the Church five years ago. I will never be like them, I'm afraid—never have the gravitas of those blessed by generations of faithful parents and grandparents whose faith flowed like a fountain, making religion more than a Sunday thing.

Still, I know that I am called to share my experience as a Catholic-come-lately, if only because there are mothers like me—mothers who have been raised with a weak moral compass, or none at all—who've discovered something missing. Mothers who've seen that parenting skills don't come naturally for those who grew up without the spiritual and emotional support it takes to raise a woman ready to be a mom.

I remember the moment I first came to grips with my deficiencies as a mother and realized that I could change.

It was 1980 and I was a single mother living in Marin County, California, with two daughters, Samantha Sunshine and Jasmine Moondance—both part of my hippie heritage. After years of exploring every nook and cranny of the counterculture and ending up a mess, on March 17, I rolled out of my waterbed, fell to my knees, and called out for God's help—though I had no idea who God was. Too hip to go to church with those "stupid Christians," I turned to Alcoholics Anonymous (AA) for support.

My life began to change as I learned to live without drugs and alcohol one day at a time. Most importantly, I was given tools (in the form of the Twelve Steps[1]) that enabled me to surrender to a "Higher Power," stop blaming others, face my shortcomings fearlessly, and work hard to overcome them.

Perhaps the most glaring of those shortcomings was this: After having sworn all my life that I would not turn out like my mother—a divorcee whose problems with alcohol, money, and men kept her way too distracted to be much of a mom—I had indeed turned out exactly like her. Despite securing a superior education, I had put my own "freedom" first, which meant problems with drugs, alcohol, money, and men. My daughters had lived in the same state of helpless and hopeless confusion that I had. How could I have done that to the little girls I loved?

AA—and this gift of soul searching it taught me—was really the beginning of my becoming a new creature in Christ, although I wouldn't know Jesus for seven more years. Clean and sober at thirty-two, I sought counseling to deal with the demons of my past, demons I'd been running from since I took my first drink at age fifteen: a father who left to pursue his dreams, making nightmares of four other lives; a mother who never really recovered; constant shuffling between relatives and a foster home; sexual abuse; and poverty. In the end, this damaged child grew into an adult unequipped to do anything but repeat the cycle.

Though the hurt I'd caused others was staggering, after making amends to my daughters for my neglect, I turned to the future, determined to become a better mom. I remember sitting on a bench at the neighborhood playground like an anthropologist—studying mothers with their children, trying to glean their secrets. I began watching and listening to myself for unconscious habits—when my actions and words were reflections of my mother—so I could turn them around for the better.

One moment stands out vividly. Three years into my sobriety, I'd met and married a younger man I felt was my soul mate. Like me, Tripp was a New Age seeker, a child of divorce, and he was ready to do something positive with his life. We married on January 2, 1983, and began building a family and home, one we wanted to be happy, healthy, and free of the baggage we carried—kind of like a Norman Rockwell painting.

A few months into the marriage, I felt like Cinderella, pinching myself to see if this new life I found so fulfilling was merely a dream. I loved preparing for a new baby, being home when my girls came in from school, cooking dinner each night. After years of chaos, my life finally felt right.

But I still had much to learn.

One day Jasmine came home from second grade, jumping like a jumping bean, tugging at my maternity top, begging me to bake a cake for the school's cake-decorating contest.

"Honey, I'm just not that kind of mother," I said. And that was the truth—or at least it always had been. As a wild and crazy single mom, I just hadn't made room in my busy going-nowhere life for this sort of thing.

Suddenly, Jasmine's shoulders slumped as though a heavy cloak had fallen on her. I knew that resignation myself from all the times my mom said no to the things the other moms were doing because it wasn't part of her lifestyle or self-image.

Suddenly, I got it. I wasn't bound by my past—not by the old ideas based on how my mother had done things, nor by how I'd done them up to now. I was free to change.

"Well, maybe we could give it a try," I said tentatively. And when I saw Jasmine's shoulders lift and the sparkle return to her eyes, I grew more full of purpose.

"What kind of cake were you thinking of?"

She wanted Garfield. And so the next couple hours became a flurry of cake mix, frosting, and orange coconut until at last a Garfield sat smugly on a foil-wrapped board, ready to take on his competition. Sensing some significance, Tripp took a picture, which is among my prized possessions to this day.

The next day, when Jasmine and I proudly carried our Garfield cake into her classroom, I must admit I felt just a little inadequate when I saw the extraordinary efforts of the Super Moms who'd been doing this for years.

The recognition we received was humble: fifth place—not for the entire school but just for second grade. Still, to me it was as triumphant as Olympic gold, and today I know that from God's perspective it meant so much more. It showed him I was willing to learn and willing to grow—and though it would take a few more years for me to know him, God used this challenge to encourage me to tackle this project of becoming a good mother with hope and joy. Now, thirty years later, I can't believe how much he changed me once I admitted how much I needed to change.

Today, as a mother of twelve—including four with Down syndrome (three adopted after our son Jonny was born)—I've done many things I never would have dreamed possible. I know it wasn't because of the Garfield cake, but because of God, who picked me up by the shoulders and gave me the shaking I deserved.

It wasn't a punishment but an invitation to change, and I will always be grateful for the second chance I was given to learn how to be a good mother, and then—like icing on the cake—to pass on what I've learned to others on a similar journey of learning to get it right.

But I'm getting ahead of myself. At the time, I had no idea where my life was going.

Several months after the famous Garfield cake, our first son, Joshua Gabriel, was born. And then, in no time I was pregnant again, even though I was using birth control. As a young father who'd just taken on responsibility for two daughters and a new baby, Tripp had mixed feelings when I told him the news. But three months into the pregnancy, when I'd begun hemorrhaging while at the bank and had been rushed to the hospital, he changed his mind. Suddenly that baby was the most important thing in the world.

Though I was hospitalized twice, we didn't lose our second son. It was a gratefully accepted wake-up call that showed us how important each life is. Not a burden, but a blessing.

After Matthew Raphael was born, Tripp and I felt we could no longer use birth control; we felt that the spiritual purpose of our lives was to continue raising a healthy family. I remember kneeling together and promising God (who at that time was only a mysterious spiritual force we felt when we meditated daily) that we would trust in him/her to provide for our family. Of course, we were thinking about material challenges, but God had other plans.

Eighteen months later, Benjamin Michael was born. However, while our material needs were being well provided for (through a series of miracles, we had been able to buy a house in Marin County and build a thriving business) and on the outside our life looked idyllic, our marriage was falling apart.

Business concerns, finances, child-rearing, in-laws, even something as trivial as how we packed the car for vacation—so much to argue about, so little time! I was so sick of fighting that I secretly began plotting to kick Tripp out of the house so I could raise our five children on my own.

But then, once again, God intervened.

Because of my desire to become a better mom, I listened each morning to a popular parenting program on a Christian radio station, promptly turning it off the second it was over so I wouldn't hear any other silly Christian stuff. After a particularly bitter fight one morning with Tripp, I tuned in a little late, just barely catching a reference to a marriage conference with a track record of restoring broken relationships.[2] I decided this would be my last-ditch effort to make our marriage work. An hour later, I had us signed up. Two days later we were driving to a fancy hotel in San Francisco, fighting all the way.

Did it work? I'll say it did, although I don't think I really expected it to. Twenty-six years later, I still thank God, through the Holy Spirit, for the still, small voice that—even before I knew him—kept patiently nudging me toward his light. Because that conference held the moment that would be the most important turning point in my life, though others would lead up to it and others would follow.

That important moment was the moment I committed my life to Christ, beginning a process that continues to this day of learning to live up to the Scriptural admonition: "He must increase, but I must decrease" (John 3:30).

Here's how it happened: The first night of the conference, we were given a workbook that contained a chart showing "The World's Plan for Marriage" and "God's Plan for Marriage." My own view, and Tripp's as well, lined up perfectly with the world's: marriage as a 50/50 proposition with the goal being "my" happiness.

When confronted with God's view of marriage as a relationship surrendered to him, I had to admit that for all my relentless spiritual work, I was still the same selfish creature I'd always been. In fact, the problem had been exacerbated by the New Age belief that I was the center of the universe. And with Tripp believing the same thing about himself—well, let's just say that no matter our noble intentions, with two gods living under one roof, our plan was never going to work.

But there *was* a plan that would: God's plan, which we were introduced to the next morning through the simple, evangelical, bring-them-to-Jesus formula known as The Four Spiritual Laws, briefly stated thus:[3]

- God loves you and has a wonderful plan for your life.
- You are separated from God by sin.
- God sent his Son, Jesus Christ, to die for you to bridge that gap.
- You need to make a decision.

Though Tripp and I considered ourselves spiritual—our house was filled with pictures and statues of great spiritual masters and gurus, including Buddha, Krishna, and even Mary and Jesus (and isn't it so like Satan to convince seekers like me that all gods are equal?)—I had never heard that Jesus was God's Son. With a degree in philosophy, I preferred complexity, so it seems miraculous that God cut through my confusion to impress me with this simple truth. And yes, indeed, I did want (head bowed, eyes closed) to ask Jesus into my heart!

With that silent prayer, I burst into tears. Glancing sideways at Tripp, I saw that he was crying, too. Something had clearly shaken us to the core. Though we'd been through various New Age initiation ceremonies, we knew what had happened to us here was deeper, more profound, more real. But having grown up without Christianity, we had no context, no understanding. We were sent off with encouragement to begin reading the Bible, starting with the Gospel of John.

We began talking about Jesus as though he were our best friend. Others wondered what had gotten into us this time, assuming it was just another of our endless enthusiastic phases. And yet, as the days and weeks rolled by, it was obvious we had experienced a change that permeated every aspect of our being.

With no advice from anyone, we felt compelled to get rid of all our New Age books, tapes, statues, and pictures. Not even wanting to pass them on—instinctually understanding that if Jesus was the truth, these things were lies—I didn't even take them to Goodwill, but instead dumped them in the trash.

We found a dusty Bible on our decimated bookshelves and began to read John, as the conference leaders had suggested. Here at last was the truth—I could feel it in my bones. My seeking days were over; I had been found. The peace that passes understanding was mine. I had so many other feelings—excitement, fulfillment, curiosity, joy—and yet all blended into peace. I was where I should be.

It was in the pages of John that Tripp and I stumbled over the verse: "Verily, verily, I say unto thee, except a man be born again, he cannot see the kingdom of God" (John 3:3, *KJV*).

While other Scriptures in this book will be from the Catholic RSV Bible, I've used the Protestant King James Bible here because it is key to my story. Not only was this the version we were reading, but the words "born again" jumped out of the text and into our hearts as the explanation for what had happened to us.

"We've been born again!" I remember saying to Tripp, absolutely dismayed. "That means we have to go to church with all those born-again people!"

My opinion of born-again people wasn't very high, as I've mentioned before, even though it was based on nothing other than my own criteria of cool. But once I had surrendered my life to Christ, cool didn't matter. I had acquired a character trait I'd never had before: submission. I couldn't explain then how I sensed what was the right thing to do, but the guidance seemed clear and irrefutable. Looking back, I know it was the "still, small voice"—the Holy Spirit—and I thank God again that since the beginning, he has always led me from within.

On our first visit with our children to an evangelical church, we were surprised by how wonderful it felt to gather with others who believed in Jesus and read the Bible. We loved the hymns and the sermons and the kind and generous people we met. Some of them had grown up in Christian homes doing daily devotions and now had children of their own with whom they carried on the faith, not just on Sunday but every day. These people had what I wanted—an expression we used in AA to discern who was good company and who was not. Tripp and I glommed on to families we could look up to and try to emulate.

We had a lot of catching up to do, and we knew it. Finally on the right path, we spent only the barest amount of time wondering why it took so long for us to find it. We focused more on the fact that, looking back over our family trees, there was little good to pass on. With only a couple of exceptions (Tripp's great-great uncle and aunt who were still missionaries in their nineties, for example), the generations before us had been marked by divorce, abandonment, alcoholism, homosexuality, disbelief, disappointment, and despair.

Why had God chosen us? I honestly cannot say. To think that I had not only survived my hardscrabble background but was now a mother with five little souls in my care, to think that Tripp could change the legacy of abandoning fathers to one of steadfast love—it was quite overwhelming. We saw our historical families as a stream going nowhere, with the great surprise being that now God had given us a chance to turn our family legacy into something special.

We realized that while we could never be carbon copies of the families that had been strong Christians for generations, we could work to become the best possible parents we could be in order to provide the spiritual foundation for our children that hadn't been provided for us. Our family's legacy would be changed forever.

It was a huge responsibility, but we were excited by the opportunity God had given us to make a difference in the future.

We haven't been perfect. How could we be, two people with the amount of baggage we have? Tripp was twenty-eight when we married, and I was thirty-four, but emotionally we were teenagers, since that's when we had started using drugs and alcohol to anaesthetize ourselves from the hurts of our childhood. As sober adults, we'd only had a few years to grow up, and so the early years of our marriage were spent working through issues that many people have already worked through—things like my anger and Tripp's irresponsibility.

But the shifting sands were gone, and now our marriage was built on the solid rock. How can I convey my joy on hearing the parable about building on a firm foundation for the first time, along with and all the stories which explained so well why things worked or didn't work in my life? Those who have grown up with the Bible may not understand how exhilarating it is for a person like me to hear them for the first time as an adult and understand why life never made sense before knowing Christ.

Every one then who hears these words of mine and does them will be like a wise man who built his house upon the rock;

> and the rain fell, and the floods came, and the winds blew and beat upon that house, but it did not fall, because it had been founded on the rock. And every one who hears these words of mine and does not do them will be like a foolish man who built his house upon the sand; and the rain fell, and the floods came, and the winds blew and beat against that house, and it fell; and great was the fall of it.
>
> —Matthew 7:24–27

So here we were, on the road to healing and advancing at an accelerated pace. We could see that God had a plan for our marriage, because even though we didn't know him, evidently he wanted to give us a head start by building our home himself. Hadn't he left his fingerprints all over the first five years of our marriage in the names of our sons: Joshua Gabriel, Matthew Raphael, Benjamin Michael? And what about our decision to trust him completely with the size of our family?

It's ironic now that the pro-life piece was there from the beginning. Today as a Catholic, knowing that God was always, always reaching for me, I might wonder why I would spend twenty years as an evangelical before finally coming completely home to the one true Church with which he has gifted us. But since God allows things to happen for a reason, I accept this as part of his plan for me: two born-again experiences—the first as an evangelical Christian and the second as a Catholic.

With that first experience, everything I thought I knew was illuminated, and many of my attitudes and beliefs shifted 180 degrees. Somehow I now knew reincarnation was not true. As a fierce feminist, I had fought for abortion rights (and even had one myself); suddenly I saw abortion for the evil lie it is. Homosexuality, which I had condoned and even briefly experimented with, was clearly wrong. My radical political hatred for my country and tradition was replaced by understanding and gratitude.

It wasn't just a turning *away* from evil; it was a turning *toward* good. My role as a wife and mother became clearer and dearer to me. More and more, I found that setting aside my own desires and serving others brought me the greatest joy. Even housework took on a spiritual aspect; I would think of Jesus washing the disciples' feet as a picture of the humility of spiritual leadership.

Eventually, I began to homeschool our children—another place where I sensed the leading of the Holy Spirit. Despite my disadvantaged childhood, I'd been a good student (or maybe because of it, as I sensed it was my ticket out of the lower class). I'd even been a National Merit scholar and managed to attend some college. But most importantly, when Samantha was a baby, I'd read a book by Maria Montessori called *The Absorbent Mind*, and I been so impressed with her understanding of children that I'd gone back to college and then the Montessori Institute in Washington, D.C., to get my teacher certification. As it turned out, I would only teach in the classroom for three years—one year with poverty-stricken children in D.C. and two years with middle-class kids in California.

Who knew that I would one day be a mega-mom, using Montessori ideas 24/7? It's things like this that make me know in my heart how much God loved me even when the circumstances of my life (through the sins of others or my own sin later on) kept me so far from him. How could I ever stop giving thanks?

That spirit of giving thanks to God with my life was very real, and I guess that's why it was easy for me to translate the concept of surrendering my life to Christ into everyday decisions and everyday life. I had lived many years for myself; now I lived for him, specifically through serving the family he had so graciously given Tripp and me.

By 1993, we had four more children (including our son Jonny, who has Down syndrome), and we moved our classroom into the largest room in the house—an acknowledgment that for now homeschooling really was the heart of our family. When other moms began asking how I managed to teach at different levels and was able to avoid the chaos associated with toddlers, I realized that my Montessori training had prepared me for motherhood in a unique way. I began to offer workshops for other mothers.

When I came across an annual Christian writers' conference a few hours from my home, I decided to attend, hoping to write a book on using Montessori principles at home. I eventually wrote that book and eight others for evangelical publishers.[4] I also began writing articles and columns for magazines and newspapers.

In the meantime, Tripp's tree company, which we had started on a shoestring shortly after our marriage, was thriving, but we were feeling increasingly uncomfortable living in a place where only 2 percent of the population attended church, and families like ours were in short supply. I had moved to San Francisco in 1972 to escape the traditional culture of Virginia, and now as a Christian I yearned for a more comfortable place to bring up our family.

In 2002, we sold our business and home and returned to Virginia with twenty-two native Californians, including Samantha and Jasmine, their husbands, and their children. Through God's grace, my daughters had been able to forgive me for my mistakes. They both had become Christians and were building faithful homeschooling families of their own. It was an unexpected blessing that they wanted to follow us across the country, but they were seeking God's will, too.

In Virginia, I felt led to put my children in public school. This was nothing I could explain logically, but over the years it has proved to be another place where I could be useful as a reporter/communicator.

School Choice: The God Factor

With twelve children, plus all-over-the-map school experiences, I've met more moms and dads than most. In public schools, private schools, and homeschooling groups, I've found hundreds of parents with good intentions who want the best for their children. And occasionally I meet parents who are sure that what's best for their children must be best for everyone else.

I had a similar attitude when I began homeschooling twenty-two years ago. On meeting a mother whose six children were scattered between a Catholic school and being homeschooled, I found myself fuming, "Why doesn't she just homeschool them all?"

As if it were any of my business.

Over the years, I mellowed. I began to understand that if God has a plan for each child's life, he will probably whisper it in the ear of each child's parents, not in mine. And we all have plenty to do keeping up with our own children's needs without worrying about everyone else's.

For those contemplating teaching at home but who are wary of an all-or-nothing approach, rest assured that homeschooling is not a twelve-year commitment; it's an option you are free to move in and out of depending on your child's and family's needs.

When our mostly homeschooled family first moved to a rural area, we found that our local public school was not only wonderfully traditional, but so stable that the first grade teacher was herself a graduate, and the kindergarten teacher was teaching sons and daughters of former students! Liberty School was clearly the social hub of the community. Since we wanted to meet people and feel connected, we enrolled a few of our children.

How could I explain this decision to someone convinced her way is the only way? Only by what I call the God Factor. It is, after all, his prerogative to have us do things we don't always understand and may even have trouble explaining to others.

My recommendation to parents trying to make the right choice: Keep gathering information, and don't forget to pray. Remember that God has a plan for each of our children. Our job is to find out what that plan is and then do our best to carry it out—one year at a time.

In 2005, I began blogging as a way to connect more immediately with my readers. Beyond the gratification of seeing my ideas in print and my name on a book or in a magazine, what I really wanted most was a trusted relationship with mothers with whom I could share my ideas. While I'd always written as though talking to a friend over a cup of coffee, the immediacy of the Internet made that even more possible. And while I was initially concerned that blogging would detract from my "real" writing, with the many beautiful relationships that have blossomed from it, I can't say that one is more real than the other. And my own ideas have grown and developed through the input of other moms.

Because of my writing, I received requests for speaking engagements. Many of them were for pro-life groups. I also had many writing assignments involving pro-life activities that frequently involved the combined efforts of Catholics and evangelicals. Like many evangelicals, I was very prejudiced against Catholics: They worshipped saints, prayed the rosary, didn't read the Bible, and followed the pope. I didn't consider them true Christians, and I judged their Church to be dead.

And yet...

And yet, through my interviews with leaders fighting Planned Parenthood, everyday heroes keeping vigil outside abortion clinics, and invitations to pro-life banquets where I met Catholics who sacrificed greatly by living a more humble lifestyle in order to support pro-life ministries, seeds of doubt were being planted in my preconceived ideas about who Catholics were.

There was also the fact that Tripp and I were 100 percent pro-life, from cradle to grave. I did not understand how evangelicals who claimed so loudly to put their total trust in God refused to trust him with their family size. While some evangelicals have thrown out their birth control and consider it non-biblical,[5] it is far from the norm. We had been fortunate—after nearly twenty years and ten churches—to find a Bible church dominated by a pro-life way of thinking.

We were attending that church in 2007 when I was asked to speak at a pro-life banquet in Maine. Since these events were usually a mixture of evangelicals and Catholics, I always challenged the non-Catholics to reconsider what it means to be pro-life: "If you consider yourself pro-life but are using birth control, then you are not pro-life at all, but simply anti-abortion as the media labels us. In this area the Catholic Church has been authentic and consistent where evangelicals have compromised for their own convenience."

But this time, something new popped out unexpectedly: *"And I think that to stop being a hypocrite, I'm going to have to become Catholic."*

A collective gasp went through the room—perhaps the loudest coming from me, as I was more surprised than anyone. Later, the evangelicals kept their distance while Catholics pressed rosaries into my hands, promising to pray for me. I would need those prayers, because the ensuing months would prove to be some of the most challenging I'd ever faced.

The next Sunday I got up early to attend the church I had identified as my local parish: St. Francis de Sales in Purcellville, Virginia. Sitting alone in the pew, I approached the Mass as a believer in Christ who'd been taught that Catholics had it all wrong. And yet, the realization that the Church had it right all along welled up in me so profoundly that I could not deny it. The biggest surprise was the amount of Scripture—from the Old Testament and Psalms to the New Testament and Gospels. I'd always been told that Catholics never read the Bible. We loved the shift from a forty-five-minute sermon that interpreted a small passage in Scripture according to the pastor's point of view to the Liturgy of the Eucharist.

I was filled with awe that, through time and space, I was united with Catholics everywhere—that we were all hearing the same Scripture and celebrating the same Mass.

Sitting alone and unknown, I had a second born-again experience that morning, as so many things were illuminated for me: the priesthood, the apostolic succession, the importance of ritual and tradition. Just as in my first born-again experience, I could not have explained much theologically; I simply felt the call from God and I accepted. Although it has turned out not to be an easy road (socially, professionally, and family-wise), not a day goes by that I am not grateful.

But that's another story, for another time. What's important here is that Tripp and I, along with six of our children, became Catholic. In the years that followed, I stepped away from writing books because I realized that I didn't know as much as I thought I had. Instead, I continued the more humbling journey through parenthood that begins as children grow up and start making decisions for themselves.

Today, I feel ready, willing, and able to write this book. I'm grateful for the opportunity to share all I've learned in the hopes that others might find more hope and meaning in parenting and be able to spend less time worrying about problems later and more time avoiding them now. Which is why, in the end, I guess I'm the right author for this book. As our culture has been corrupted and the once taken-for-granted agreement on moral values destroyed, parents find themselves more on their own. Many, like me, who have grown up with inadequate parenting and/or a lack of spiritual foundation are trying to pick up the pieces.

Jesus told us that he didn't come for the healthy, but for the sick (see Luke 5:31). By sharing my story, I hope the message rings loud and clear: We are all mothers in the hands of a merciful Father. God doesn't need much to work with if only we are willing to put our lives in his care. If he can take a loser like me and make something worthwhile, he can do it for anyone.

And if you ask him, he will.

CHAPTER TWO

Purpose-Driven Parenting

"It is easier to build strong children than to repair broken men."

—Frederick Douglass[6]

"Are those *all* your kids?"

Now that most of my twelve kids are grown and I'm no longer wandering the aisles of grocery stores with five or six in tow, I don't hear those words very often.

I miss them. I miss the *Make Way for Ducklings* days when my sweet progeny trailed behind me like I mattered more than anything in the world. Even with half a dozen still at home, I feel a lot like an "empty nester."

How grateful I am to have had so many children! How grateful I am that even before I became Catholic I gave up my "zero population growth" philosophy and opened my heart to the possibility of children. Despite my own unhappy background, somehow I intuited that the real path to growth and healing for someone like me lay in producing a happy family—with all that entailed in becoming a better mother. After all, you can't go back and give yourself a happy childhood, but in providing one for others, you can come awfully close.

Along the way, in the midst of countless dinners, diapers and doctors' appointments, I discovered something our culture has in large part forgotten: Children are not a burden but a blessing. That's a paradigm shift for parents in a culture bombarded by messages like this one from *Forbes* magazine:

Have $235,000? That's What It Costs to Raise a Kid Today—Before College [7]
Take your pick. Would you rather buy a 2012 Ferrari or would you rather have a baby? The choice is yours but the cost for each is about the same.

A report out today from USDA reveals that a middle-income family with a child born in 2011 can expect to spend about $234,900 ($295,560 if projected inflation costs are factored in).

And that's just the first seventeen years!

My goodness, what prospective parents wouldn't be intimidated, especially if they don't have faith in something more substantial than conventional wisdom. Is it any wonder so many take charge of their reproductive potential by limiting their family size? With the current cultural imperative to "have it your way"—to focus on eternal youth and self-fulfillment through food, fashion, and fun—sadly, even many Catholics justify their decision as common sense.

I was thirty-seven years old, expecting our third son, when I began to feel revolted by birth control. I wasn't a Catholic and not even yet a Christian. All I had going for me was questioning the status quo. And though my babies (five of them, including the two daughters I brought into our marriage) had cost me my figure and more-needed-than-ever sleep, though Tripp and I had less time and money to spend on ourselves, and though we worked harder than we ever dreamed possible, I had found a joy I never felt possible also.

> **Children Are a Blessing**
> Behold, sons are a heritage from the Lord, the fruit of the womb a reward. Like arrows in the hand of a warrior are the sons of one's youth. Happy is the man who has his quiver full of them! He shall not be put to shame when he speaks with his enemies in the gate.
>
> —Psalm 127:3–5

And now, especially with grown children who have children of their own, the years have proven again and again what I only caught a glimpse of when Tripp and I took that leap of faith and promised God (in the limited way we then understood him) that we would trust him with our family size.

I know of couples who didn't catch that glimpse in time. Let me share one story.

A Vasectomy Tale

Theirs was a story like many others: cradle Catholics who'd known each other since parochial school, fell away from their faith in college, married at twenty-two, and returned to the Church after the birth of their first child eighteen months later.

But they returned to the Church on their own terms, still using about abortifacient (euphemistically known as "birth control") pills. As Mark Faas recalls, "We were Cafeteria Catholics, for sure."

When their daughter was joined by a brother three-and-a-half years later, Mark surveyed their new normal—a wife worn out at the end of the day, twenty minutes to pack two kids in the car—and decided two kids was plenty. Bragging to his friends, "My kids will be out of the house by the time I'm forty," he didn't tell his family until the day before his vasectomy, barely eight weeks after the birth of his second child.

In the meantime, Mark and his wife, Jen, continued to go to church and began to attend Bible studies. Just six months later, Mark was at a men's retreat when his conscience kicked in: "What have we done here?"

Trying to right their wrong, the Faases turned to adoption. Still, they were haunted by the enormity of their mistake: "We had spit in God's face and the gift he had given us. Knowing we had committed a mortal sin, we went to confession. The priest did not let us off the hook, instead telling us, 'This is a mortal sin, and you must get it fixed.'"

The vasectomy had been covered by insurance, but a reversal would not be. It would cost thirty thousand dollars. Mark then got a tip from a friend about a surgeon who had made a ministry of vasectomy reversals: Loddie Roeder of New Braunfels, Texas, charged only three thousand dollars. Mark journeyed there for the procedure in June 2009, but month after month his wife did not get pregnant.

Still, their family rejoiced in December when they brought home a new baby girl—with a heart defect they would eventually correct—from China.

When fertility tests revealed Mark's sperm count was nonexistent, he made a second pilgrimage to Texas to give the reversal another try. A year later, October 2011, Mark and his wife welcomed their fourth child, their second son. They hope for many more.

How the world has tricked so many good people, convincing them that children are a burden they should try to limit or avoid! How many of us have been deluded into thinking that anything—material comfort, playthings, convenience, financial security—is worth more than the most precious gift God has given us? How could we accept the word of the world over the word of the Lord?

Hooray for people like Mark, who are unafraid to admit a mistake and do what it takes to correct it. And hooray for a God of forgiveness, grace, and second chances!

It takes a lot of faith to do that kind of backtracking, especially when your friends and relatives think you're nuts to waste your money on the opportunity to take on more financial obligation. But couples like the Faases are the blessed ones, as is anyone willing to set aside fear and grab hold of faith. This is really the foundation on which your family will rest. Decades hence at holiday celebrations and reunions as you look around the table at the faces of your loved ones, you will know that you have more than the family *you* planned—you have the family God planned specifically for you.

By then you will have undoubtedly discovered that what the world teaches is wrong. And perhaps you will agree with me when I say: Children are a resource richer than any man can discover, mine, or develop. Worth every sacrifice of time, money, and energy. More valuable than anything else I could ever produce on my own. The only meaningful stake in the future. Children will be my offering when I stand before my Heavenly Father, hoping to hear, "Well done, my good and faithful servant."

If we listen hard enough, he just might give us a little glimpse of that heavenly reward here on earth. I had one of those glimpses last year, shortly before my daughter Maddy graduated and married the man of her dreams.

Maddy (child number nine) and I decided at the last minute to surprise big sis Sophia (child number seven) at college to catch an opera recital she had thought we were too busy to attend. We drove for four hours, growing more excited with each mile at the anticipated delight. Finding our way through the music department, we turned a corner and saw Sophia at the end of the hallway in full makeup, wig, and costume. I will never forget the expression of joy on her face as she ran to throw her arms around her little sister and then me.

In a testosterone-dominated family (eight sons, four daughters), it's always refreshing to have some girl time. After popping my buttons with parental pride while hearing Sophia sing, then waiting for her to reappear from backstage as her simple self, we treated ourselves to Chinese food, shopped for the starving student at Goodwill and Walmart, and finally settled down in her humble room for a chick-flick on her laptop.

When the credits had finished rolling, Sophia took her two-layer bed apart and laid the single mattresses side by side so the three of us could share a full-size bed on the floor, with me in the middle of a sister sandwich. Maddy fell asleep instantly, but Sophia—who's always been a more tentative sleeper—lay beside me in the dark, pouring out her heart about school, her friends, and her hopes for the future. The experience was so beautiful I could scarcely breathe. I was thanking God for the years of sacrifice—the sleepless nights, dirty diapers, and home-school math—which had somehow earned me these mystical moments enwrapped in the most intimate thoughts of my grown up little girls.

And then Sophia said something I'll never, ever forget: "Mommy, I love you so much. Thank you so much for having a big family. I love my brothers and sisters so much. I know you and Dad sacrificed a lot to have all of us, but I can't imagine life without all of them."

Any parent, no matter the size of their family, will understand what I mean when I say that my heart nearly burst with joy. These are the words of affirmation all of us long to hear someday from our children: a recognition that, though there were times of hurt and misunderstanding, we were on the right track. This is a joy I could never have experienced had I not long ago surrendered my life to God and taken seriously my calling to be a mother.

The world teaches us that children come with a cost, and they certainly do. But the world doesn't realize that they also come with a reward: the harmony created in a home centered on God and his purposes—a home where children aren't brought up to "do as I say," but to "do as I do."

If we want children to live intentionally—that is, with purpose and meaning—then as parents we must live that way, too. If we want children to be obedient to God, then we must be obedient to God. If we want children to live with faith, then we must live with faith ourselves. If we want our children to find joy in a faithful life, then we must find it, too.

My message here is this: An obedient, faithful, and joyful life is within the grasp of any parent who wants it, no matter what their background or religious pedigree.

And it starts with surrendering your own plans in exchange for God's.

While I know that birth control is not an easy topic—even for Catholics—it must be the starting point. And no matter where you stand right now, I hope you are willing to think and pray about it.

This is not meant to impose a guilt trip on you. We all have our limitations and challenges, and we are all in the process of overcoming as we learn to walk more closely with God. Relying on his plan for our individual families and following the Church's teaching on birth control requires a lot of faith, and for that reason, I don't presume to judge anyone for decisions they make in this area. One thing I appreciate about Catholicism is that the teachings are there, but no one is watching over your shoulder to admonish you for doing the wrong thing. God has given us all free will, and it is up to us to learn to exercise it more wisely as we grow.

My observation that purposeful parenting begins with trusting God with the size of one's family is not meant to *indict* but to *invite*. I love nothing more than to share the joy Tripp and I have found in the twenty-some years since we surrendered—and to encourage those who haven't yet surrendered in this area to reconsider. Our children (whether through birth or adoption) have brought us greater joy than anything else we have done, and I can't imagine life without any of them.

I'm thinking that one of the reasons they turned out so well is not because they were brought up under a rigid religious code, but because they had parents who questioned the status quo and then let go of fear in favor of faith.

I have a necklace I wear all the time with silhouettes of children's heads—eight boys and four girls—in order of their birth. Each one is engraved on one side with a name and on the other side with a birth date. Tripp started this necklace for me after Ben (number five) was born, and he has faithfully added to it with each new baby. It has sparked countless conversations, during which (for some reason) many have opened their hearts to tell me that one of their deepest regrets is not having more children themselves.

Often someone says, "I would have loved to have had more children, but my husband (or wife) didn't want to." I've met people who have lost a child unexpectedly when it is too late to have another. I've met only children who speak of the loneliness they feel, as well as the looming responsibility of caring for two parents on their own. My heart breaks for those who live with the unexpected consequences of decisions made long ago.

But for all those who have told me they wish they had had more children, I've never met anyone who said they wished they had fewer, which is why I encourage parents to think and pray for God's will rather than their own.

No Experience Required

What do we know when we begin having children, anyway? Are any of us really prepared? Do we have the right answers to the all the questions parenthood will hold?

Isn't it ironic? In our culture, you have to buy a license to fish, pass a test to drive, and jump through some pretty tough hoops just to adopt a stray kitten at the pound. But when it comes to raising children (unless you're adopting) none of us have to do a single thing to qualify.

What a curious thing this parenting business is, where lack of experience, training, or knowledge doesn't matter at all! The greatest responsibility in the world—the care and nurture of body, mind, and soul—is dropped into the lap of just about anyone, regardless of worth or character, regardless of timing, circumstances, and even sometimes—unfortunately—the willingness to receive.

What was God thinking? Our heavenly Father, the perfect Parent, delegating to the most important job in the universe to such imperfect representatives!

Perhaps he was leveling the playing field for a moment, giving each of us the opportunity to step outside our foolish, selfish ways to learn to live for someone else.

Do all parents rise to the occasion? Certainly not. But we all have a chance to. When a woman discovers she is pregnant, she often starts immediately to do her best to improve her baby's circumstances. She gives up caffeine and alcohol, takes prenatal vitamins, and prepares to minimize the trauma of birth. She creates an environment to meet the baby's needs and prepares herself by reading books. Some even change their music habits—nothing like harp concertos to soothe a fretful baby (or the whole family, for that matter)! But how much a parent allows children to impact his or her life varies from person to person.

Last night, while trying to take my mind off my broken leg (yes, I am writing this book with a broken leg!), I indulged a guilty pleasure by watching more reality TV than I'd ever admit were I not bound to transparency as a writer. One show was a contest involving four houses, with a prize to the person whose decorating skills were judged the best. One of the competitors was a brazen, busty blonde in tight pants, a teensy spaghetti-strap top, and five-inch platform heels that— especially in my own recovering state—filled me with fear for her safety. She was covered in tattoos from her neck to her wrists. She was definitely pushing fifty, too.

Believe me, with my own past I lean towards compassion rather than judgment when it comes to this kind of thing. As a young pagan mother, I was pretty much on the same trajectory. I'm thankful that God got hold of me sooner rather than later! But the point I want to make is this: In the tour of her house, which included a room-sized closet filled with two hundred pairs of platform heels and a gorgeous but family-unfriendly kitchen, there was no sign that a child lived there. I didn't give much thought to this until the final awards scene when a sweet, tousle-headed son—maybe six years old or so—hurtled out the front door to jump into the arms of his mother, almost knocking her off her precarious balance, because he was so proud.

Clearly, his parents were intent on carrying on their lives as they had before the arrival of their child. And why wouldn't they be? Doesn't our society urge us to not let having kids keep us from enjoying glamour and fun?

I am so grateful that at some point I completely surrendered to motherhood and allowed myself to change to fit the needs of my calling. After forty-three years of parenting—with four still at home, one in college, and adult children who need me once in a while—I can say with gratitude that my children have been the greatest instrument of change in my life. Were it not for them I would not be the person I am today—but instead, still stuck in the selfish, self-centered ways of my past.

"It's Not About You"

I'm borrowing these four words from the opening salvo of *The Purpose-Driven Life* because, frankly, I can't think of any better phrase that sums up the challenge of parenting.[8]

While I never read evangelical pastor Rick Warren's thirty-million-copy bestseller, my oldest daughter, Samantha, said I didn't need to: "Mom, you could have written it!" How well she knew my mothering style! I guess it was my endless preaching to my children ("Where one or more are gathered, there Mom will give a sermon") to transcend their natural self-centeredness and learn to put others first.

And so, while I can't vouch for anything but Warren's first sentence, I will say that not only is it a reference point for me as mother in the thick of parenting, with all the large and small choices that entails, but it has also served as part of the ethical code I work hard to instill in my kids.

The birth control issue may be the first and most difficult parents face—and please know that we're friends even if you're not quite there yet—but no matter where you are in your parenting journey, you've probably encountered many more that you never anticipated. Choices that made you hesitate or squirm, choices that brought you to your knees, choices that brought out the good, the bad, and the downright ugly in you.

> There are moments when, whatever the attitude of the body may be, the soul is on its knees.
>
> —Victor Hugo, *Les Miserables*[9]

None of us is perfect, and this adventure in parenthood—which, remember, requires no preparation or qualification whatsoever—is strictly on-the-job training. Perhaps a few sweet ladies come into it so unselfish that they are good to go, but my guess is that most of us are somewhere on the spectrum between Melanie and Scarlett in *Gone with the Wind*. In the beginning I leaned toward being very, very Scarlett. God led me, one baby step at a time, to put the needs of others before my own.

But don't kid yourself. Melanies have their issues, too. They may become hung up with maintaining a perfect image: homeschooling, cooking meals for shut-ins, sewing their children's clothes, and so on. That kind of giving is wonderful. But let's face it, giving that we plan in advance and that the world sees is not the most difficult kind.

Where the rubber hits the road is how we behave when the unexpected comes along: when you're whipping up that lasagna and your toddler knocks the ricotta cheese all over the floor; when you're running late and your tween daughter has a clothes meltdown; when it's Friday night and you've earned your downtime, but your son suddenly needs his soccer uniform washed for the game tomorrow morning.

It's not the things we initiate that test where we rate on the selfish-o-meter. It's the things that take us by surprise that no one else will ever see. It's night after night of broken sleep, new shoes for them but not for you, cleaning up from a family-wide stomach flu, having to settle for G-rated movies for a decade or two, wishing for more time to hang out on Facebook or Pinterest, and having to make a mad dash for poster board before the store closes at nine.

My advice is to make peace with the fact that your life is not your own—sooner rather than later. As you let go of impatience, annoyance, and frustration (all symptoms of selfishness), you will feel your burden lighten and your joy increase. And if it's true that "when Momma ain't happy, ain't nobody happy," then it must be equally true that when parents are happy, our families are happier too.

> Selfishness in all its forms is directly and radically opposed to the civilization of love.
>
> —Pope John Paul II

The fact is that we are born as selfish creatures—look at any want-my-way-and-want-it-now toddler to see what I mean—but it's a condition we can grow out of. Our job as parents must be to work hard to make sure we don't end up with "want-my-way-and-want-it-now" teens, who will be crippled with selfishness for life.

Kids are quick to spot hypocrisy, though. You can't preach against selfishness while acting even a teensy bit as though the world revolves around you. Be quick to confess to your children when your selfishness has interfered with the harmony of the home, and they will begin to take more responsibility for their own.

And they'll have more respect for you, too.

More Difficult Today

Doesn't it strike you as strange that for thousands of years parents raised children without the benefit of books telling them how to do it?

In the '50s child-rearing books were written by pediatricians like Dr. Benjamin Spock and Dr. T. Berry Brazelton. Now with the growth of blogs and self-publication we find mothers of one or two who claim to be experts on everything from diapers to diet to discipline!

And how about those parenting gurus with programs that claim to be the only righteous way? They sweep through mostly evangelical churches (often with crossover into Catholic ones as well), appealing to well-intentioned parents but imposing rigid templates based on the idea that God made us all from cookie cutters. Their one-size-fits-all philosophy may work for some but not for many, which leads to misunderstandings and divisions within individual churches and the Church at large.

With Parenting Experts Galore, How to Choose? Try Asking:
- Is the teaching biblical?
- How much of it is "branding" or media hype?
- Does this person have the experience and qualifications to teach?
- Is she humble, authentic, willing to admit her own struggles and failures?
- Is he encouraging, while challenging you to a higher level?
- Will the teaching lead your family closer to each other and to Jesus?
- Does it resonate with the still, small voice within—the voice of the Holy Spirit?

In 1960, six parenting books were published. Now, each year I get over a hundred in my mailbox for review. Everyone has answers because everyone has questions, which makes me ask: Why are modern American parents so insecure and so vulnerable, at least when compared to previous generations? Several reasons come to mind:

- Separation from extended families, sources of help and wisdom
- Less experience with younger siblings due to smaller families
- Pressure on parents to remain cool, hip, and sexy
- Consumer forces manipulating parents through guilt
- Boomer parents doing their own thing rather than being grandparents
- Moral relativism

What I see as a positive in this bleak picture is that today's parents want something more. If their birth family was broken by divorce, they want stable marriages and will work hard to keep them. If their mothers were neglectful or their fathers distant and aloof, they want to become better for the sake of their kids. Parents today are willing to invest money, time, and energy into learning how to do things the right way.

The good news is that, as my life is a witness, *with God's help you can overcome any limitation.* He takes your willing heart and makes it grow. When it comes to becoming a better parent, he wants you to succeed.

Is God calling you to be a better parent? Do you feel unworthy? So did many people in the Bible. Just remember that God doesn't call the equipped; he equips the called. All you have to do—like so many saints who came before, and especially the Blessed Mother—is say, "Yes, Lord! Yes!"

> For truly, I say to you, if you have faith as a grain of mustard seed, you will say to this mountain, "Move from here to there," and it will move; and nothing will be impossible to you.
> —Matthew 17:20

My life is unusual in that, after many failures in those first thirteen years with my first two children, I was given a second chance with ten more—a chance to get it right, to become the mom I never had myself. And as a mom who has ended up raising two generations of teens, I can tell you from a parent's perspective that kids live in a different world today than the one occupied by the teens of twenty-five years ago. And the world they live in isn't pretty.

It starts when you've just learned to read and you're in the grocery checkout line with your mom practicing your new skills. You read "Guys Rate 50 Sex Moves," "How to Outsmart a Bitch," "Keep an Orgasm from Slipping Away" (*Cosmopolitan*, August 2012) and "Sneaky Little Things that Sex Up Your Marriage" (*Redbook*, August 2012).

But even before you can read, your education about what it means to grow up begins at the mall with Victoria's Secret and Guess and Calvin Klein. It continues with innuendo-laced TV shows. Even if your parents avoid those, there are the commercials between the family shows and football games.

And it's not just sex; it's violence. I will never forget Peggy Noonan's August 27, 1999, commentary following the Columbine shootings:

Think of it this way. Your child is an intelligent little fish. He swims in deep water. Waves of sound and sight, of thought and fact, come invisibly through that water, like radar; they go through him again and again, from this direction and that. The sound from the television is a wave, and the sound from the radio; the headlines on the newsstand, on the magazines, on the ad on the bus as it whizzes by—all are waves. The fish—your child—is bombarded and barely knows it. But the waves contain words like this, which I'll limit to only one source, the news:

> ...was found strangled and is believed to have been sexually molested...had her breast implants removed...took the stand to say the killer was smiling the day the show aired...said the procedure is, in fact, legal infanticide...is thought to be connected to earlier sexual activity among teens...court battle over who owns the frozen sperm... contains songs that call for dominating and even imprisoning women...died of lethal injection...had threatened to kill her children...said that he turned and said, "You better put some ice on that"...had asked Kevorkian for help in killing himself...protested the game, which they said has gone beyond violence to sadism...showed no remorse...which is about a wager over whether he could sleep with another student...which is about her attempts to balance three lovers and a watchful fiancé... This is the ocean in which our children swim. This is the sound of our culture. It comes from all parts of our culture and reaches all parts of our culture, and all the people in it, which is everybody...[10]

The social forces that worked to create this situation are formidable: the sexual revolution, legalized abortion, increased divorce, fatherless families, normalization of deviant behavior, pornography—and we are now two or three generations into the decline. This book isn't about what we can do to fix these problems as much as it is about what we can do to raise children in a culture gone mad.

What seems obvious is that without the support of society (that is, a cultural agreement that sex outside marriage is wrong, that modesty is a virtue, that hard work and sacrifice give life meaning, that our purpose in life is not to please ourselves but to please God), parents must work much harder than any other generation to carry children through these troubled waters.

Purpose-Filled Parenting

When I accepted God's purpose for my life at age thirty-eight, I understood that, while my life had never been without a purpose, I never really had a clue what it was. I didn't want my kids to grow up willy-nilly like that. I wanted them to grow up trusting God and finding his purpose for their lives from the get-go.

Don't confuse having a purpose with having goals. A child may want to grow up to be a doctor or an opera singer or a rocket scientist. Those are goals, not purposes. *Goals* are worldly ends we want to reach. *Purpose* is the reason behind the goals.

Many parents, thinking long-range, start college savings funds before their baby is sleeping through the night. But what's much more important than investing in a child's education is investing in his or her character. What kind of men and women do we want to produce? Having that long-range vision has been vital for me as I've guided my children through the day-to-day.

My kids have been educated in many settings: Catholic, Christian, public, and homeschool. They've been to youth groups, VBS, Sunday school, and Bible studies galore. But their dad and I are still the ones who oversee their daily life, discuss with them the practical application of their spiritual knowledge, hold them accountable, and nudge them back on track when they're a little off. We know them better than anyone. That's our job as parents.

There's a word that describes what I've had in mind since I began raising my kids with purpose: *mensch.* It's one of those Yiddish words that's a challenge to translate, but worth the effort because it's loaded with meaning. It's based on the German *mann* for man. But *mensch* means so much more. One dictionary defines *mensch* as "a person having admirable characteristics, such as fortitude and firmness of purpose." *Mensch* also signifies a perfect gentleman or a perfect lady, someone compassionate, caring, and kind.

When I think about the kind of adults I want my children to grow up to be, I'm thinking *menschen:* men and women with good, strong, and gracious character. I'm not as concerned with *what* they grow up to be career wise as I am with *who* they grow up to be. I want them to grow up to be faithful wives and husbands, loving parents, brave believers, good friends, and committed citizens.

Being a *mensch* means living a life of integrity. Integrity comes from Latin words that, when put together, mean "untouched, whole, entire." In modern English, the Collins *American English Dictionary* defines integrity as:

1. The quality or state of being complete; unbroken condition; wholeness; entirety.
2. The quality or state of being of sound moral principle; uprightness, honesty, sincerity.

Living with integrity, then, means knowing exactly who you are and always being that person—not compartmentalizing, for instance, by being Cathy Catholic on Sunday at church but living like Secular Susie the rest of the week.

To have an impact, our faith doesn't have to be shouted, just lived. When C.S. Lewis was asked how he planned the Christian allegory in his Narnia series, he replied that he started with his vision of a faun, and that the Christian elements (never stated directly) just bubbled up. In the Bible, the book of Esther doesn't contain a single reference to God, and yet it is an unforgettable lesson in faith.

> Preach the gospel at all times. When necessary use words.
> —attributed to St. Francis of Assisi

When our faith is part of who we are, it will bubble up in our lives quite naturally, too. This is what we should aim for in ourselves because this is what we want for our children as well. Going to church and CCD will never be enough to help them withstand the pressures of an increasingly temptation-filled, faith-unfriendly world.

We must do all we can to build a relationship of love and trust, helping God to capture our children's hearts and teach them the beauty of living one's faith while being in the world but not of it. This is the job God calls us to, and we can depend on his help to see us through.

For decades I've been a cheerleader for my kids, and now I'm here as a cheerleader for you. The beauty of purpose-filled parenting is that, no matter what kind of a past you've had, you can change your child's future—and ultimately the world's—one day, one decision at a time.

CHAPTER THREE

Be a Parent, Not a Pal

"When can I start dating?" Maddy asked me shortly after starting middle school.

My goodness, I thought, *she's only eleven!* But then again, since we'd moved to Virginia and switched from homeschooling to public school, I'd anticipated more salt-and-light situations like this.

Sure enough, some of her friends had started "going out"; although, as it was explained to me, "going out" isn't actually dating. It just means a boy and a girl like each other and, often through the use of proxies (as in, "Jenny, will you find out if Gabe wants to go out with me?"), officially become a couple who walk to class together, with or without holding hands, along with phone calls and texting after school. But beyond that, some of Maddy's sixth grade friends had actually started going on movie dates, enabled by a parent willing to drive them back and forth.

What's up with these parents? I thought, and then quickly reminded myself, *There but for the grace of God go I.*

Twenty-four years earlier, I was the crazy single mom with two little girls crammed into our red Karmann Ghia who strutted into back-to-school nights in *Cosmo* cover-girl garb, proud to stand out in the crowd. When Samantha (my oldest, now forty-three) went on her first date at the age of twelve, I was thrilled. Having grown up without a father, earthly or heavenly, I craved affirmation from men. A date for my daughter meant she was somebody, too.

Max appeared at our door, fresh-faced and eager, and walked her out to the car where his mom waited to chauffeur them to the movies. On returning home, Samantha reported he had been a gentleman, opening doors and surprising her with a new necklace for Christmas.

I couldn't understand why Samantha didn't want to go out with him again. But then again, Samantha always seemed to have a sense that our lives were off-track—not as fun or free as her beat-of-a-different-drum mom imagined them to be. She envied her friends with normal (that is, traditional) families.

Now, a generation later, these traditional families seem threatened with extinction, with parents as clueless as my former Cool Mom self having become the norm. While I can't speak for them all, I can share what was behind my parenting approach: Having grown up with no spiritual foundation or moral guidelines myself, I didn't have much to pass on. And since my childhood wasn't undergirded with love, I had no understanding of what parental love looked like.

During the late '60s and '70s, as a member of the counterculture, I counted personal freedom as a top priority. I ended up thinking that by giving my children a lot of freedom I was demonstrating my love.

My kids didn't even have set bedtimes.

All that began to change when Samantha was a high-school junior. She'd begun dating Kip, a boy she'd known since fifth grade, when the three of us—Samantha, Jasmine, and Crazy Cool Mom—had moved to Marin County from San Francisco. Kip remembers her bohemian city style, which stood out in a preppy suburban culture. We remember him showing up for their first date in white pants and a turquoise shirt, and Samantha coming down the stairs—in completely unplanned synchronicity—in white pants and a turquoise shirt (this was the '80s). As a friend put it, "They look like figures on a wedding cake." Five years later they would be sharing their wedding cake. But in the meantime, we all had a lot of growing up to do.

Typical of my parenting style, I had never told Samantha what time to come home. But at some point in her junior year when she started coming in from dates with Kip at two in the morning, I had to confront the obvious: Kids just don't always make good choices.

By then, Tripp and I had been married for a few years, had our first two sons, and were striving for "normal." Ready to admit that everything we thought we knew was wrong, we were also ready to make the changes we needed to make to give our kids a better start than we'd had ourselves.

Anticipating a battle (after all, exercising parental authority was new territory), we braced ourselves and set some limits for Sam. But later, passing by her bedroom, I heard her on the phone, bragging to a friend, "My parents gave me a curfew. I have to be home by midnight from now on."

The funny thing was, she sounded quite happy about the whole thing—proud, even, that her parents were doing their job. That's when I began to realize that my permissive parenting style, which I had been so confident was demonstrating my love and trust, was actually sending the opposite message: "I don't care."

Kids not only need limits, they secretly want them. Thank goodness I discovered this in time to ditch the permissive parenting and do a better job raising Samantha's younger brothers and sisters. Kids need to know someone's in charge; they want to know that their parents care enough to think through what's best for them and then stand by their standards, no matter how uncomfortable things get.

Consider this: Researchers have observed that groups of school-children on an unfenced playground tend to huddle together, too timid to venture very far. When the playground is fenced, the children, feeling more secure, spread far and wide, making every bit of space their own.

Limits are like the guardrails that keep us from plunging off a bridge. They're there to protect us—they are instruments of love, not oppression. By making clear boundaries, parents demonstrate their love while empowering their children to explore life with an assurance of well-being and safety.

Nowadays I find there are now a lot of parents like I once was, parents who think the *laissez-faire* approach ("kids will be kids!") to parenting will work. Even parents who set limits when their children were younger suddenly think they should back off when their children are teens.

On October 12, 2004, *USA Today* covered a study by Synovate, a research market firm, which found that 43 percent of parents wanted to be their child's best friend.[11]

> Some parents felt their own parents didn't understand them, and they see a best friend as someone who is fun to be around, listens and is non-judgmental…. But unlike a traditional parent, a best-friend parent "doesn't give you rules and tell you what to do," [according to Ian Pierpont, Synovate senior vice president]. One mother wouldn't make her child do homework because it would make him unhappy," Pierpont says. "The majority of best-friend parents are just not setting guidelines and rules."[12]

That explains a lot—like the times when I would call to check on my teen's whereabouts and the other parent responded like I was a weirdo.

Or when I called to introduce myself to the parents of someone one of my older sons was going out with to perhaps see if we were on the same page when it came to dating guidelines, and they sounded defensive.

What is driving this new parenting trend? Some experts think one factor involves both parents working outside the home, making them so highly motivated to enjoy their family time that they avoid anything that might create tension or conflict.

Like best-friend parents, I want to be loving and understanding. I would like to avoid tension and conflict. But I also know I have a job to do in terms of guiding my kids through these important years. Sometimes parental love must be tough.

At our local school board meeting a few years ago, I watched a father come forward with a tale of woe: His daughter had been driving friends home from a party when she was pulled over and received a DUI. In addition to her legal problem, a DUI in Loudoun County, Virginia, means a student is pulled from any athletic team. The father was pleading for an exception for his daughter, arguing/rationalizing that with two working parents and no after-school supervision at home, now more than ever she needed her team to strengthen her character.

Actually, as football coach John Wooden once said, "Sports do not build character...they reveal it." The DUI daughter had already demonstrated that being involved in athletics was not enough to keep her on the straight and narrow. Now it was a lesson she (and her dad) would have another chance to learn, but in a harder way.

Wasn't it a loving thing for that father to go before the school board to plead on his daughter's behalf for a second chance? How many parents would care enough to do the same thing?

Of course, I'm not serious. Parental love isn't based on feelings— although most of us certainly have more than our share—but on a commitment to do whatever it takes to help our children reach their potential. Sometimes what appears to be loving, particularly in the eyes of the world, isn't loving at all.

The pleading father wasn't thinking long-term about the woman his daughter would grow to become. If he were, he'd be spending his time not pleading with the school board, but reinforcing the lessons she needed to learn. What about her friends who might have been killed? He might explain to her why she needed to experience the consequences of her decisions and how she would become a better person if she accepted them in the right spirit.

That would be a truly loving response.

As a parent, I know how hard it is to see your child go through consequences that hurt. In striving for balance, I've certainly been guilty on occasion of being merciful when mercy alone wasn't warranted. But I've learned that this often delays the lesson my child needs to learn, which means that God will undoubtedly supply another opportunity for my child to learn it. Might as well get it over with sooner rather than later!

What's most ironic is that as parents are trending away from setting limits, kids are more in need of them than ever.

Consider: When Samantha was growing up in the '80s, our society pretty much agreed on what was right and what was wrong. Our kids weren't bombarded from their toddler years with sexual imagery and music. Parents trying to bring up responsible young adults weren't clashing with hedonistic worldviews that granted kids limitless license.

Even earlier, back in the days of *Leave It to Beaver* and *Father Knows Best*, while parents knew that their children were their responsibility, they also had the support from the culture. Certain behaviors, like sex outside marriage, were wrong, plain and simple. Sure, kids made mistakes, but when they did there were consequences and shame to deal with. Consequently there weren't that many mistakes.

But forty years of progress in normalizing teen sex through Planned Parenthood and the media have changed everything. Today's TV shows, music, and movies portray sex (now casually referred to as "hooking up") as easygoing fun and barely worth a second thought. TV ads for herpes medications make it clear that even an STD doesn't have to get in the way of having sex whenever you want.

Girls Who Date Early at Risk

That's the message of a twenty-seven-page report published by the National Campaign to Prevent Teen Pregnancy, incorporating research from Yale, Columbia, and the University of California. It's called *14 and Younger: The Sexual Behavior of Young Adolescents*, and you can download your own copy at *www.thenationalcampaign.org/resources/pdf/pubs/14summary. pdf.*

Among the conclusions:

- Approximately one in five kids has sex by age fifteen.
- Early dating leads to early sex.
- Early first sexual experiences for girls are more likely to be unwanted.
- Girls dating older boys are very vulnerable to early and unwanted sex.
- Sexually experienced kids under fifteen are more likely to use drugs and alcohol.
- Girls who have sex before age fifteen are more likely to become promiscuous or pregnant, contract an STD, or drop out of high school.

In our case, even as the increasing need for clear boundaries was clashing with the trend to parents as pals, Tripp and I were trending backwards—learning to set appropriate limits and to stand by them, even when our kids balked. Even when other parents acted like we were from another planet.

In today's culture, it can be difficult to be a traditional parent when other parents are way more cool. But now I understand how confusing it is for kids whose mothers and fathers aren't secure enough in their own identity as parents to dress and act appropriately. Living on the periphery of an affluent, sophisticated area, we see more than our share of facelifts, breast implants, and middle-aged women in tight Guess jeans. Our back-to-school nights feature way too many Cool Moms (like I used to be), dressed in skimpy outfits the school dress code forbids their daughters to wear.

In other times and other cultures, parents grew into their roles naturally, more concerned with raising the next generation than maintaining their youthful identity. Now a growing number sport midlife-crisis tattoos and in-your-face T-shirts. They grew up in an era where solid parents and solid families—as portrayed by Ward and June Cleaver, or the Andersons from *Father Knows Best*—were ridiculed. In a culture obsessed with youth and beauty, many adults balk at giving up their own adolescence. Parents ambivalent about growing up themselves are hardly in a position to make good decisions for their children. This spells trouble for the next generation, just when they need more guidance than ever.

So what should the role of parent look like in this modern age? Maybe a little perspective would help.

God's Design: It Takes Time

I've always found it fascinating that, throughout the animal kingdom, the young progress so quickly compared to humans. Why is it that foals and calves and lambs stand up and walk within minutes of birth, while our babies take months just to sit upright without help, and almost a year—or maybe more—to walk? Why do our children need us for so long? God made us in his image, but he could have done things differently. Have you ever wondered, as a parent in the thick of it, why we live so closely together for so long? What could have been God's intention?

He wanted relationship. He wanted the kind of intimacy and trust that come from knowing each other through and through. Knowing our children so completely takes a lot of time. But becoming refined as a parent (and therefore closer to God) takes a lot of time, too.

In the animal kingdom, development is governed by instinct. Mother and father birds feed their babies because they have to, according to the instincts with which God created them. And baby birds grow and do what they're supposed to because they, too, are governed by instincts.

Not so with human mommies and daddies and the new lives we create. We don't have many instincts other than survival (such as babies crying for food when they're hungry, or jerking our hands away from something hot). What we have instead of instincts are potentials, built into us by God, which are best released when we are brought up in loving families.

God must have had something in mind when he created us to be dependent on our parents for such a long time. After being a mother for forty-three years, and now blessed to be friends with my adult children while still caring for my last three at home who were adopted when I was already a grandma, I think he designed growing up to take so long for the sake of intimacy—in order for us to bond with and love each other more. He did it this way so we could build strong relationships with each other.

We are made in God's image, and God made us to have a relationship with him. As parents, we teach our children about relationships, from the moment we first respond to their need for food, warmth, and comfort to the time they are ready to leave the nest to begin a relationship with the world on their own.

God also built some wonderful potential into our children—potential that will help them grow to be joyful, gracious, caring, and compassionate people. While growing up, your child may have teachers, coaches, and mentors, but *you* will always be your child's primary teacher, and the work you do to build character will be far more important than any academic, sports, technical, or trade skills acquired later.

This isn't just a platitude; it's something Tripp and I learned as business owners. While at first Tripp insisted on hiring only fully trained tree workers for his arbor care company (aptly named Mr. Trees), a surprising number of negative experiences led him to conclude that it was far more difficult to instill good character into a highly skilled worker than to hire men with good character and teach them the tools of a new trade.

Character is everything, and it begins in one place: the home.

Just in case that sounds a little intimidating, remind yourself: God doesn't call the equipped; he equips the called. When you entered Parenthood 101, you entered a 24/7, on-the-job training. Do parents sometime cut class, daydream, fall asleep? Absolutely. But for anyone who wants to reach his or her own potential, the lessons never stop. Sometimes when I look back over my own motherhood, I'm not sure who really learned more, my kids or me.

God is always revealing to us more about who we are so that we can become better persons and/or parents. For example, it wasn't until Sophia, my seventh child, was away at college that I came across a key to understanding the conflicts we had when she was a teenager: the differences between extroverts and introverts. Sophia spent much of her teenage years in her bedroom, which was very unusual because I had planned our living spaces to encourage family togetherness (see chapter four). But while the rest of us hung out together in the evening, Sophia wasn't interested. Her door was always closed and she was unavailable, which I interpreted as rejection. My entreaties to come out and talk only made her more resistant.

What I didn't understand then was that, in a family dominated by extroverts, with all the ruckus that entails, Sophia was the lone introvert, and an extreme one at that. While she could rally herself to be the star of the show on stage or the life of the party with friends, she regarded her home in a different way than the rest of her clan, whose constant upstaging and vying for attention didn't stop at our front door. By contrast, when Sophia came in from a demanding day of maintaining her place on the social ladder, the last thing she wanted to do was join in the conversational chaos at home. She wanted to close her door and make the world go away.

I was left on the other side of the door, wondering why. Why was this daughter—who seemed so social to the outside world—rejecting her family at home? The fact that I'd written a few books on parenting by that time and was expected to have the answers didn't help. And to top it off (as I realized only later) Sophia's shut door touched painful places in my subconscious. As a teen, I had pounded helplessly on my mother's locked door as she would drink and try to shut out the reality of her responsibilities and regrets. Somehow I'd ended up in the same place forty years later, begging my daughter to talk.

If someone had told me my daughter was an introvert, I would have said, "No way!" She had many friends, was involved in a slew of activities, including chorus and drama. She loved singing solos and could use even the smallest role to upstage everyone else.

But what did I know? At that time the buzz about the differences between extroverts and introverts hadn't filtered its way into popular wisdom via today's backyard fence for moms, the Internet. I didn't know that the difference between extroverts and introverts wasn't always defined by their social behavior—although some introverts are indeed reserved pretty much all the time. What defines an introvert is how they recharge their batteries. Therefore, an introvert like Sophia could be "on" for hours in public, but come home and desperately need to be quiet and left alone.

In today's American culture, extroversion is considered the normal—and in a way it is, as 75 percent of the population is extroverted. In a large family like ours, this translates into rambunctious conversations and interruptions galore. An introverted family member not only has a hard time being heard but has to spend a lot of energy just hanging out with the family.

Had I known and understood, I could have helped Sophia understand herself, for surely my thinking there was something wrong with our relationship only made things worse. And her craving for solitude spilled over into neglecting her chores as she resisted my ongoing campaign to pry her out of her room. With just a smidgen of maternal understanding, I know now we could have begun a conversation that would have led to acceptance and compromise: X number of hours alone; X number doing laundry. And Sophia would have blossomed just through being accepted and appreciated for who she was.

HOW TO CARE FOR INTROVERTS [13]

- Respect their need for privacy.
- Never embarrass them in public.
- Let them observe first in new situations.
- Give them time to think. Don't demand instant answers.
- Don't interrupt them.
- Give them advanced notice of expected changes in their lives.
- Give them fifteen-minute warnings to finish whatever they are doing before calling them to dinner or moving on to the next activity.
- Reprimand them privately.
- Teach them new skills privately rather than in public.
- Enable them to find one best friend who has similar interests and abilities: encourage this relationship even if the friend moves.
- Do not push them to make lots of friends.
- Respect their introversion. Don't try to remake them into extroverts.

—Linda Kreger Silverman, PH.D.

Instead we had some rocky times. The good news is that through it all we had the Lord—and we made it through. As soon as I understood why things had been so difficult for us, I explained this to Sophia and asked for forgiveness, because the bottom line is this: The burden is on the parent to understand and grow. And although I can't hit the remote and rewind those years, I can look forward to basking in the utter joy I'll feel when I watch my sweet daughter's motherhood unfold from the birth of her first child in a few months through all the plans God has in store for her.

Maybe it helps that, as a mother with a sketchy history, I was forgiven for some grievous mistakes. And while at first on my new journey as a believer, I expected to be perfect, I quickly discovered I would never be. What was I to do about the mistakes and misunderstandings I was responsible for, even as I did my best to walk with God?

First I came to this conclusion: Parenting is the most important calling in the universe, and God gives parents approximately twenty years to build faithful, loving men and women of character, while making the most of their own. Because of this, Satan (the Great Divider/Discourager) will do all in his power to destroy or at least warp families by alienating children from their parents and parents from their children.

Since no parent is perfect, every parent will make mistakes. Sometimes—as in the case of my struggle with Sophia—it may take a long time to figure things out. Sometimes pride keeps parents from admitting they were wrong. In the meantime, the Great Divider—who can take something big and make it appear small, or take something small and make it appear big—will whisper in our children's ears, building a case, accusation upon accusation. He will also do his best to sear parents' hearts with every mistake made, to discourage them from continuing to try.

What if we snatched this destructive template from the enemy? What if we committed to bringing up our children in an atmosphere of self-awareness and discovery—theirs and ours—where we counted on the Holy Spirit to lead us from trials to triumphs? Once Sophia and I acquired the understanding we needed to respect each other, it was as though we had blasted Satan to smithereens (in the Looney Tunes sense of the word), and we were more united than ever as mother and daughter.

How to resist the enemy? The keys are *curiosity* and *communication*:

- What else do I need to learn to become a better parent?
- How can I equip my children to raise families when their time comes?

While I've mainly addressed parents who need encouragement to step up their skills, to learn to blend love and authority, I also want to warn against heavy disciplinary styles that are long on legalism and short on grace. Some parents who grew up without much structure may, as a reaction, seize such a program (a few of which have developed almost cult-like followings). The parental authority and control pushed by these programs leave no room for individual differences. The leader of one popular, one-size-fits-all program has only two daughters and no sons. In a world where God created men and women differently, how could someone with no experience raising sons presume to present himself or herself as an expert? Another leader prescribes rigid discipline techniques that actually have resulted in the deaths of adopted children with problems greater than their unseasoned parents could have possibly anticipated. Both of these "experts" claim their approaches are biblical.

What I don't like about legalistic, one-size-fits-all programs is the idea that as parents we are finished products, ready to impose the correct system on our kids so they will turn out as well as we have. There's no discussion of the work parents need to do to continue their own learning process as they learn to listen for the still, small voice; let go of pride; surrender to God; and humbly acknowledge that they are still in the process of refinement themselves.

As a parent, you're meant to speak with confidence and authority (not authoritarianism), but you also need to listen with an open heart for corrections God may have for you, both large and small. Flexibility and the ability to change on a dime when a change is called for is required, but you also must have steadfastness, remaining unswayed by any fears of losing your children's love.

Will there be moments when things get uncomfortable? Yes, there will; perhaps there may even be moments when you think a relationship is lost. But with God's help you can find your way through and maintain your children's respect. Remember that someday your children will be parents, too—facing the same challenges. It helps to remind them of this, showing them the bigger picture and explaining the decisions you make so they won't have to buy a shelf full of parenting manuals when they grow up!

The challenging moments are easier if your family has a solid foundation of love. Remember that old adage, "The family that prays together, stays together"? It's an old adage because it's true. Beginning and/or ending your family's day with devotions (even just a hymn, a Bible verse, and a prayer), praying a daily rosary, or reciting the thrice-daily Angelus together will change the whole atmosphere of your home.

Including God in your family discussions and decision-making and teaching your children to find words of comfort or rebuke or challenge or joy in the Bible are practices that not only build each of you up as individuals but also build your unity as a family.

Finally, for children to respect parents enough to trust that what they tell them is best, parents must live lives of integrity. The Domestic Church (what the *Catechism* calls our homes, which shows how important families are) is not a "Do as I say" but a "Do as I do" world. The responsibility of parents is enormous. But when you feel inadequate, just remember that if you ask, God is sure to give you all you need to be a worthy parent to your children—after all, they're his children too!

CHAPTER FOUR

Mastering the Media

Ever had a guest you wish you hadn't invited? Maybe you were looking forward to a little fun and ended up feeling that you'd wasted a lot of time instead. If so, maybe you'll tune right in to the picture of this ungracious guest.

He dominates the room, grabbing attention whenever he can.

However, a little attention is never enough; he's always demanding more. He monopolizes time and conversations, making it difficult to get a word in edgewise. His voice is too loud; his manners pathetic. He swears and takes God's name in vain, has little respect for family ties, pokes fun at things that matter deeply, and tells off-color jokes in front of the kids.

Yet he's one of the most popular guests in town. Despite his atrocious manners, his calendar is full—all day, all night, weekdays, weekends, rain or shine, in sickness or in health.

And he doesn't discriminate. You'll find him in the poorest homes and the richest, among the happy and the miserable, all ages, races, and colors.

Maybe you've spent some time with this ill-mannered guest yourself. Maybe sometimes you wish you hadn't.

Somehow he seems to mix up your priorities. You find he's rubbed off on you, putting words into your mouth—or your children's—that weren't there before. You hear family members being sarcastic or mean to each other. You find yourself distracted from the ideals you've set for yourself. So why do you continue to entertain this guest?

Why do you keep turning on the tube?

It's a question every parent needs to ask, especially those who may have grown up in homes with too much TV and too little guidance. Since we tend to continue the habits with which we were raised (unless we consciously question them), this is another area where we need to evaluate ideas and make good decisions.

The fact is that in the United States our children watch an average of twenty-one to twenty-seven hours of television per week. And while much has been researched and written about the negative impact of so much TV, there has been little change in these figures over the years. On the contrary, however, TV has spewed forth ever increasingly graphic depictions of violence and sex, with less and less regard for children and family sensibilities. There have also been forces at work to use entertainment to push political agendas that promote behaviors once considered taboo—TV as a tool of social engineering.

Granted, television has a lot to offer educationally—from toddlers learning letters, numbers, and shapes to teens learning about everything from the Civil War and robotics to Shakespeare's Catholic roots. But the truth is that TV is chosen less often for education than for entertainment, and it's the entertainment that needs closer scrutiny than ever.

Gone are the days of *The Brady Bunch* and *Little House on the Prairie*; these are the days of *Desperate Housewives* and *Jersey Shore*. You may not watch TV yourself (who has the time?), but you need to understand what's going on and the role it's playing in your children's lives. Even if your family is TV-free or TV-limited, your child is trying to cope in a world of peers whose ideas, opinions, and behavior are based to a large extent on what they are watching and talking about.

Reality Check: How Much Are They Watching?[14]

1. Average number of hours per week that American one-year-old children watch television: 6

2. Number of hours/week recommended by the American Pediatric Association for children two and under: 0

3. Number of minutes per week that the average American child ages two through eleven watches television: 1,197

4. Number of minutes per week that parents spend in meaningful conversation with their children: 38.5

5. Average number of hours per week that the average American youth ages twelve through seventeen watches television: 20 hours, 20 minutes

6. Hours of TV watching per week shown to negatively affect academic achievement: 10 or more

7. Percentage of time children ages two through seven spend watching TV alone and unsupervised: 81

8. Percentage of day-care centers that use TV during a typical day: 70

9. Percentage of parents who would like to limit their children's TV watching: 73

10. Percentage of four- to six-year-olds who, when asked to choose between watching TV and spending time with their fathers, preferred television: 54

11. Hours per year the average American youth watches television: 1,154

12. Hours per year the average American youth spends in school: 900

How Many Murders Did You See Today?

The American Psychological Association has concluded that the average child watching two to four hours of television a day will witness 8,000 murders and 100,000 other acts of violence before graduating from elementary school.[15]

What are the effects of watching all this violence? Is it harmless, as some contend? Or if it is harmful, how can harmfulness be measured?

In one study conducted at Pennsylvania State University, one hundred preschoolers watched twenty to thirty minutes of television three times a week for four weeks. Half the children watched cartoons with lots of violence; half watched shows with none.

Only four to six hours of viewing spread out over a month—yet researchers found a clear difference between the two groups of children.

Those who watched violent cartoons were more likely to hurt others, argue, and disobey than those who watched nonviolent programs.[16]

This study is typical of research throughout the country, which verifies that television violence makes viewers more prone to aggressive behavior in real life. One seventeen-year longitudinal study found teens who watched more than one hour of TV a day were almost four times as likely as other teens to commit aggressive acts in adulthood. [17]

The fact is that the level of violence—the number of incidents per hour and the graphicness of its depiction—is increasing all the time. The Parents Television Council, a nonpartisan education organization advocating responsible entertainment, had this to say in its *State of the Television Industry Report: TV Bloodbath: Violence on Prime Time Broadcast TV:*

> Entertainment violence is a slippery slope. With repeated exposure, even the most gruesome and grisly depictions of violence eventually seem tame. In time, viewers become

desensitized, so Hollywood has to keep pushing the envelope in order to elicit the same reaction.

Lt. Col. David Grossman, author of *Stop Teaching Our Kids to Kill,* explains: "Violence is like the nicotine in cigarettes. The reason why the media has to pump ever more violence into us is because we've built up a tolerance. In order to get the same high, we need ever-higher levels...the television industry has gained its market share through an addictive and toxic ingredient."[18]

Yet, despite the mountains of research, the consensus of the medical community, and a growing list of casualties from copy-cat crimes, Hollywood continues to produce increasingly graphic and gory entertainment products, all the while denying any culpability for the violent behaviors their products inspire.[19]

Well, you may be thinking, *I keep my kids away from violent shows.* But violence is only part of the problem. What has had a broader and even more devastating impact is TV's obsession with sex.

Everybody's Doing It

Remember Joe Camel? He was the iconic camel caricature reintroduced by R.J. Reynolds (RJR) in 1988 on Camel cigarette packs and in ads. In 1991, a study showing that children were as familiar with Joe Camel as they were with Mickey Mouse accused the tobacco company of deliberately targeting children. In a lawsuit, San Francisco attorney Janet Mangini alleged that in the three years since Joe Camel appeared on the scene, the brand's yearly sales from teenage smokers had shot from $6 million to $476 million.

Central to the litigation were internal documents which clearly documented RJR's long-term marketing plan: imprinting children with an image that would pay off when they were old enough to smoke, and pushing that decision earlier. A 1974 internal memo noted the need to reach kids early because "virtually all [smokers] start by the age of 25" and "most smokers begin smoking regularly and select a usual brand at or before the age of 18."[20]

So what does smoking have to do with sex? Everything, when it serves as a parallel to illustrate how irresponsible and destructive the entertainment industry has been in promoting more and more sex— and more *extreme* sex, making even the most deviant seem normal and casual and fun.

It's not just cable shows about polygamy and fetishism, either; I'm talking mainstream. I remember anticipating the new television series *Glee*. As a family full of musical kids who'd grown up singing in chorus and dancing in shows, we all were looking forward to a show we could enjoy together, one we could maybe make a weekly event. But after a promising start, the show quickly degenerated into yet another vehicle for the Hollywood message that all sex is good—gay sex, teen sex, casual sex, adulterous sex—and that the only evil is people who don't get it (that is, Christians).

Was it a funny show? Was it charming? Was it attractive? Were there some good lessons to be gleaned, particularly on acceptance and incorporating those with physical and social disabilities? Yes, indeed there were. But unfortunately, the good was inextricably bound with the evil—you had to swallow both or none at all. Our family opted for none at all.

Does that sound extreme? Well, look at it this way: Would I invite a guest to come into my house and sit down with my kids to tell them how wonderful and fun it is for teens to have sex when and where and how they please? That it's okay for their mothers and fathers to have affairs with co-workers or neighbors? Would I give my blessing to anyone—no matter how charming or funny—to spend a few hours a day telling my kids that everything their dad and I had worked so hard to teach them, along with the words of the Bible, the *Catechism*, and their priests, was wrong? Why would I sabotage my own work as a parent? If I believe that God's plan for human sexuality is best, why would I jeopardize my children's future well-being and happiness?

"But it's entertainment. It's just fun. It can't make a difference...". I can hear the words of protest because many of us are so programmed to turn off the real world and tune in to the tube. It's like the proverbial frog. You know the story: If you throw a frog into a pot of boiling water, he will immediately jump out, but if you start him off in comfortable water and keep raising the temperature, he will never notice until it's too late to notice at all.

Like that frog, we have become desensitized to the danger surrounding our children. We don't see that the garbage our kids are watching—no matter how clever, smart, or entertaining—is fundamentally different than the innocuous shows we watched when we were young. Unless we take a step back and look at TV content from God's perspective, and with an eye to how it works to destroy the good we are trying to build into our children's lives, we just won't get it.

Evil isn't always ugly. It can masquerade as beautiful—so alluring it requires a supreme act of will to resist it. We must begin with the recognition of what is evil and a refusal to compromise just because something is fun or entertaining. This is a value we need to learn to exercise ourselves as well as teach our children, especially considering that if the temperature of the water has increased since we were young, it will only continue to increase for our children and grandchildren.

We need to make hard choices. Guarding our kids' health involves more than keeping them from seeing ads for cigarettes. It's their emotional and spiritual health that will be at risk when they start imitating the sexual license they see on TV.

And just in case you think they *won't* imitate it, the scientific results are in (see insert).

Does Watching Sex on Television Influence Teens' Sexual Activity? [21]

- Watching TV shows with sexual content hastens the initiation of teen sexual activity.
- Sexual talk on TV has the same effect on teens as depictions of sex.
- Shows with content about contraception and pregnancy can help to educate teens about the risks and consequences of sex—and can also foster beneficial dialogue between teens and parents.

But it's about even more than violence and sex.

Who Are We Really?

In chapter two, I emphasized the importance of having a vision of the men and women we want our children to grow to be, specifically using the Yiddish word *menschen* to describe something for which we lack a specific English word: gentlemen and ladies of unquestionable character.

But there's another value that's very important to me: authenticity. I want my children to be genuine and sincere—not false or copied, but the real deal.

Television is the great leveler. Unlike books, which stimulate a reader's imagination, TV provides all the sight and sound needed to keep a passive audience enthralled. It's this passive enthralled audience that TV delivers to advertisers, which we'll look at in depth in chapter five. But here I want to discuss the social ramifications of cradle-to-college TV programming for youth, with specific channels galore for children of all ages and shows that many children watch daily while their parents are either too busy or too trusting to monitor. Even as the American Academy of Pediatrics has continued to discourage the use of media before the age of two,[22] many children are already accustomed to passive TV viewing time when they reach toddlerhood. And while many shows do offer some educational value, they still become part of a pattern of usage that will be ingrained in the psyche of the child: TV not only is entertaining, it features many of my best friends (Dora and Blue and Clifford) and certainly most, if not all, the answers.

Then the child becomes a tween, now depending on Nickelodeon and Disney shows to teach her what's hot and what's not—how the cool kids dress and talk and act in school and at home. Certain vocal patterns and slang become part of the tween/teen culture, a culture which is increasingly shaped by the media and advertising.

What every parent should find worrisome is the lack of freedom our children have to become the individuals they have the potential to be. Where certain stereotypes are deemed cool and others are not, children will gravitate toward the cool. If the cool kids are sassy and have a lot of attitude (rolling eyes, back-and-forth head thrusts, and in-your-face behavior), then nothing we can do will convince them otherwise.

There's also the problem of mainstream programming: popular shows aired during family hours but filled with coarseness, crude jokes, and sexual innuendo. Not to mention sarcasm, disrespect for authority, and the demeaning of others. Isn't it interesting that *programming* is a word that refers to both TV schedules and brainwashing?

If viewing violence leads to violence, and viewing sexual license leads to sexual license, then surely sitcoms driven by low standards drag our own standards down. Why invite a guest with such terrible manners and insensitivity into your home night after night?

"Bad company ruins good morals," according to 1 Corinthians 15:33. As parents we warn our children to be careful in choosing their friends. Shouldn't we also be more concerned with our children's authenticity? For those who watch a lot of television, a question begs to be asked: "How much of who you are is who you *really* are, the person you were meant you to be? And how much is who you've become because of what you've been watching?" If our children's role models are the teeny-boppers on the Disney Channel, there's not a lot of room for them to realize their own God-given potential.

Maybe it's time to take a TV break and, as a family, figure out how to become more intentional in your viewing habits so God can use this to bring out the best in you rather than the worst.[23]

After all, it's *your* home and you're in charge of the guest list!

Larger Than Life

First of all, let me just say: *I love movies!* During my wild-and-crazy years in San Francisco, I loved going to musty old repertory theaters that screened classic, foreign, and cult films—a different double bill each night. After moving across the Golden Gate Bridge to Marin County and marrying Tripp, I was thrilled to find someone who loved movies as much as I did. But as our family grew rapidly, it was one of those things that just slipped away.

Tripp and I came into our marriage in 1983 TV-free. For the many reasons I've shared, we didn't see any reason to change, especially since we wanted to raise children with good manners, who spoke without sarcasm or putting others down. We wanted our children to grow up to be sincere and real.

Busy building our business, raising our children, keeping up with all the books we wanted to read, I don't remember feeling any lack in our lives. But I will never forget the thrill I felt when Tripp came rushing in on December 31, 1986, announcing: "Barbara, there's a machine you can buy that plays old movies, so you can watch them anytime you want!"

An hour later we were at The Video Store, an obviously hastily built little shack down the road in Larkspur, to find out more. Since we didn't own a television, we needed a screen, so we invested in a monitor and our very own VCR, then rented our first two movies to celebrate New Year's Eve: *West Side Story* and *Some Like It Hot*.

There weren't many movies to choose from back then. Still, Tripp and I felt like we'd died and gone to cinema heaven. Generations have grown up used to being able to watch whatever, whenever, and they take this kind of freedom for granted. But when it was new, it was profound. And for a family with no TV that could now watch Disney together—well, like I said: cinema heaven.

Since Tripp's and my taste in movies could be pretty edgy (because we were still locked into our cool image), we had two kinds of movies: those we watched with the kids and those we watched after the kids were in bed. I mention this because, while it seems self-evident, I have too often seen parents with young children at the theater, watching movies saturated with violence, sex, or coarse humor—and more than once I have seen fathers in video stores picking out slasher movies with elementary-age kids.

> And he said to his disciples, "Temptations to sin are sure to come; but woe to him by whom they come! It would be better for him if a millstone were hung round his neck and he were cast into the sea, than that he should cause one of these little ones to sin."
>
> —Luke 17:1–2

I couldn't imagine what these parents were thinking—until my daughter Samantha (the victim of my own poor judgment during her early years) reminded me that I took her to see *Alien* when she was ten. Shame on me, and shame on me whenever I forget that "there but for the grace of God go I." All we can do is pray for today's parents and their children. Who knows? Maybe back then someone in that theater prayed for Samantha and me.

Once Tripp and I were married and had set our sights on raising a healthy family, we were instinctively careful with what our children saw. But we always had plenty of choices; the truth is, there's a wealth of uplifting and positive movies out there which can be part of the heritage you pass on to your children.

A lot changed again in 1987 when we became Christians. We didn't need anyone outside telling us our movie habits had to change—we just knew. That's the power and beauty of the Holy Spirit, the still, small voice within us that we can choose to obey or disobey. Tripp and I chose to obey.

Over the years, I've found it important to not rely on the MPAA ratings to judge the content or quality of movies. Take a noble movie like *Glory*, which tells the true story of the first black regiment to fight for the Union in the Civil War—it's rated R while the latest, most ultraviolent Batman sequel, *The Dark Knight Rises,* is rated PG-13. The inspirational movie *The King's Speech* is rated R for brief profanity, while "comedies" filled with the lowest, coarsest, most anti-woman humor around are rated PG-13, which supposedly means they are OK for kids.

Parents need to know that it takes more work than glancing at MPAA ratings to properly guide their kids' movie habits—but the good news is that there are resources to help.

"But Everyone Else Is Seeing It!"

I'm not sure what my kids have been expecting all these years when they throw down this opening-night-at-the-movies gauntlet. Perhaps their renegade mom will suddenly come to her senses? "Why, sweetheart, what in the world was I thinking? You know how much I've always wanted to be like all the other parents. Of course, you can see the movie!"

Yeah, right.

One of the disadvantages of having a mom who's raised two generations of teenagers is that I've been studying movies and reading reviews for forty years. Which means I know too much and care too much to let my kids see just anything—whether everyone else in the world is piling into theaters to see it or not.

Don't get me wrong. This isn't a rant against Hollywood. I love movies and always have—from the first time I plunked down my fifty cents at the humble movie place down the road to see *Rio Bravo* to last month when I shelled out eleven dollars per ticket at the palatial suburban Cineplex for *The Hunger Games.*

In the intervening years, though, more than the price of a ticket has gone through the roof. Remember when movies like *Ben Hur* and *The Sound of Music* won Academy Awards? Now you're more likely to find winners like *Mystic River* and *The Departed* than occasional friendly fare like *The Artist*. Times have changed, and movies have changed with them. Or is it the other way around?

For anyone who buys the tired old argument that movies simply reflect the culture, here's some food for thought from Paul Harvey: "Nobody could have persuaded a generation of Americans to produce a baby boom. But Shirley Temple movies made every couple want to have one. Military enlistments for our Air Force were lagging until almost overnight a movie called Top Gun had recruits standing in line."[24]

If movies don't shape the choices we make, then why in the world do business titans throw millions of dollars away to imprint names on our entertainment-saturated consciousness? And why do anti-smoking advocates raise a ruckus when stars smoke on screen?

It seems a no-brainer that kids exposed to coarseness, foul language, impurity, and despair are vulnerable to shedding the morality with which they've been raised. And why are parents of teens and tweens willing to sabotage the work they've done for years to build their children's character?

So, yes, I really do care what my kids see. And since Hollywood has continued to push the envelope—and since the MPAA ratings just don't cut it with me—I have to do my homework.

And so when I get the ole Everyone Else refrain, I drag my kids to the computer, click on a trusted site for a review, and start reading it aloud, looking for the embarrassment factor.

If you struggle with the Everyone Elses, you can try this too. It has a way of wrapping up the movie debate pronto.

Here are my favorite sites:

- Catholic News Service—catholicnews.com/movies.htm (in conjunction with the former U.S. Conference of Catholic Bishops film site; helpful Catholic rating system)
- Common Sense Media—commonsensemedia.org (family-friendly reviews and ratings for movies, TV shows, and books)
- ScreenIt! — www.screenit.com (morally neutral, very detailed reviews)
- Plugged In—www.pluggedinonline.com (a Christian site aimed at parents of teens with lots of media savvy)

More Than Entertainment

The entertainment industry is about more than entertainment. Movies and TV are also about social engineering—spreading enlightenment through stories and the characters who inhabit them. This explains the rapid ascent of homosexuality—once universally regarded as an aberration—to a place of almost complete acceptance among young people and complete confusion when it comes to the clash of their church's teachings on marriage and the pressure on those who resist the bandwagon.

But think about it: how many TV shows have at least one sympathetic homosexual, and how often is that character the wisest, most caring on the show? Not to mention shows like *Queer Eye for the Straight Guy*, with a whole crew of loveable gay guys: What's not to love? And on the other side, there's often a Christian caricature whose stupidity and meanness only increases sympathy for the gay guy: What's not to hate? Thus, a generation of Catholic kids has grown up hearing one thing from their church (at churches where the truth is preached) but constantly encountering media prejudice and misunderstanding about their faith, not to mention the peer pressure of a propagandized generation.

More than ever, kids need parents who are firm in their faith and in the teachings of the Church, and who are unembarrassed to defend both. Parents need to understand the forces at work to manipulate public opinion, and they need to explain them to their kids.

As I mentioned, in our early years of family formation, Tripp and I did not own a TV. In 1986, we got a VCR. Then, with the advent of satellite TV, we opted in. At the time, we were homeschooling, and the many new stations promised great educational treasures in history, science, and so much more. We made the decision to block the major networks so that coarse sitcoms and crime shows were still not part of our children's formation.

We also set up our home to reflect our priorities. Especially with the rise of the Internet and individual computers, we saw the importance of emphasizing family togetherness rather than individual entertainment.

Limit Media by Encouraging Family Togetherness

• Reorient your home so that bedrooms are for sleeping and changing clothes.

• Move desks, computers, and TVs out of bedrooms.

• Reorganize your family room to accommodate all computers and study places.

• Have only one TV the whole family watches together, or just one extra for younger sibs.

• Make dinner preparation fun so everyone will join in the kitchen chatter.

Tripp and I had an advantage when we finally brought a TV into our home: We had never gotten into the habit of just flopping on the couch and flipping channels to relax. We only turned on the TV when there was something worth watching. For families committed to becoming more purposeful in their TV habits, I recommend a similar shift. Many parents have no idea what imaginative children can come up with when they are not dependent on TV. My adult sons have thanked us for their TV-free years and the happy memories of outdoor and indoor adventures they created for themselves.

My best advice today is balance. The truth is that there is a great deal of educational, informative, noble, inspiring, and uplifting material in movies and on TV. But like all good things, it requires intelligence and moderation to keep the proper perspective. As in so many other areas, it falls on us as parents to be purposeful in our choices, and to teach our children too, so that we are not mastered by the media but are masters of it.

CHAPTER FIVE

Consumer-Proof Your Kids

Someone's out to get your teens—and they mean business. They're the movers and shakers, the behind-the-scenes team backing the brazen, ill-mannered guest exposed in chapter four—the one monopolizing the time and shaping the thoughts of so many families. And really, no one is safe from this insidious influence, because even if you've carved out a cultural oasis for your family where the ignoble is ignored and the focus is on the finest, your children are surrounded by peers whose families are unaware of or uninterested in the damage to character and values under the guise of entertainment.

One of the standards I've asked my kids to remember when they're tempted by movies and TV shows that aren't egregiously wrong but just coarse and unbecoming, is this: "Would you feel comfortable if Jesus were sitting next to you while you watch? Because, actually, he is."

> Finally, brethren, whatever is true, whatever is honorable, whatever is just, whatever is pure, whatever is lovely, whatever is gracious, if there is any excellence, if there is anything worthy of praise, think about these things.
>
> —Philippians 4:8

Against the Giants

But there is something even more important that we need to teach our kids—an awareness of the cultural forces aiming to turn them into consumers who can be manipulated into buying products, ideas, and even politics through shameless exaggeration and lies, relentless indoctrination, and propaganda techniques.

The outlines of the campaign for your child's soul are documented in a 2003 PBS *Frontline* special called the "The Merchants of Cool," a tip-of-the-iceberg look at the aggressive marketing used to control how American teens spend their money.[25]

At 25.6 million strong, today's generation of American teens represents the hottest consumer demographic ever, with far more spending power than their boomer parents had—topping $200 billion in 2011.[26]

Some examples:

Television marketing executive: "Teens run today's economy. There's an innate feeling for moms and dads to please the teen, to keep the teen happy, to keep the teen home. And I think you can pretty much take that to the bank."

Teen market researcher: "[Teens are] given a lot of what we call guilt money. 'Here's the credit card. Why don't you go online and buy something because I can't spend time with you?'"

Part of the problem is the monopoly within the entertainment industry. Five mega-corporations—"the true merchants of cool"—control what is being sold to the youth culture: Rupert Murdoch's Newscorp, Disney, Viacom, Universal Vivendi, and AOL/Time Warner. With multiple venues (TV shows, music, movies, live performances), each can cross-promote their products, creating a blizzard effect.

Mark Crispin Miller, communications professor at New York University, explains why these companies spend millions on teen marketing research and how that research is implemented:

> The MTV machine does listen very carefully to children. When corporate revenues depend on being ahead of the curve, you have to listen, you have to know exactly what they want and exactly what they're thinking so that you can give them what you want them to have.

Now, that's an important distinction. The MTV machine doesn't listen to the young so it can make the young happier. It doesn't listen to the young so it can come up with, you know, startling new kinds of music, for example. The MTV machine tunes in so it can figure out how to pitch what Viacom has to sell.

Parents need to understand—and explain to their kids—what they are up against. According to Robert McChesney, communications professor at the University of Illinois:

> The entertainment companies, which are a handful of massive conglomerates that own four of the five music companies that sell 90 percent of the music in the United States—those same companies also own all the film studios, all the major TV networks, all the TV stations pretty much in the 10 largest markets. They own all or part of every single commercial cable channel.
>
> They look at the teen market as part of this massive empire that they're colonizing. You should look at it like the British Empire or the French Empire in the 19th century. Teens are like Africa. You know, that's this range that they're going to take over, and their weaponry are films, music, books, CDs,

Internet access, clothing, amusement parks, sports teams. That's all this weaponry they have to make money off of this market.

The outcome of this fierce competition among the media giants is that programming content continues to become more sensational, more crass, more pornographic.

As Crispin-Miller notes:

When you've got a few gigantic trans-national corporations, each one loaded down with debt, competing madly for as much shelf space and brain space as they can take, they're going to do whatever they think works the fastest and with the most people, which means that they will drag standards down.

Some parents may already be hip to the fact that the water temperature in the cultural pot they swam in when they were teens has risen to the point where their own little tadpoles should not even go there. They may have given up TV altogether, or they may monitor it closely, blocking channels like MTV. But there are still a lot of parents out there operating under the assumption that TV is no more dangerous or corrupting than it was when they were kids.

The fact is that being a parent takes a lot of work: not only cooking, cleaning, shopping, but also overseeing education (and you don't have to homeschool to feel the demands of schedules, supplies, and studies), chauffeuring kids to extracurricular activities, keeping up with dentist and doctor appointments—you know what I mean. Who has the time—or the desire—to sit down and watch The Disney Channel or Nickelodeon with their kids?

Yet, as a parent, watching is a must, for when you do, you will find reason for concern. I hope this quick peek into the consumer-driven madness of kids' TV will sound a wake-up call to take control of this aspect of your children's lives: an alternate universe built on marketing research and manipulation that counts on captivating the most vulnerable demographic—a universe that actually seeks to indefinitely prolong the me-first! mode of childhood and delay spiritual maturity.

And that's the point, isn't it? Because if a child begins to see things from a higher perspective—shifting from me-first to God-first—he will be less putty in the hands of marketers. Hence, the deliberate dumbing down of our culture to keep us buying—nurtured in childhood, raging in adolescence, and hopefully becoming the status quo of our adult lives.

Teenagers: A History

Would it surprise you to learn that the word *teenager* is a recent addition to our language? So is the concept of the teen years as a separate stage between childhood and adulthood. While there is some debate over when it was first coined, it is generally agreed that the first instance in print was *Reader's Digest* in 1941.

This is an important starting point for parents seeking wisdom in dealing with teenagers in today's world. The assumptions we make about these years and our role in them are based on some very manmade constructs about what the maturation process would have looked like without the interference of politicians, educators, social engineers, and now—most damaging of all—the merchants of cool who own the teenage years.

Let's start with agrarian societies, where children worked alongside their families, with lessons in between from mothers, grandmothers, aunts, and older sisters. Some children attended one-room schoolhouses, learning all they needed to know by the eighth grade. In many ways those were simpler times, but lest you scoff at our forebears for their lack of learning, consider that perhaps they just had need of a different skill set.

Take, for instance, this eighth grade final exam from Saline County, Kansas.[27]

Graduation Examination Questions of Saline County, Kansas
April 13, 1895
J.W. Armstrong, County Superintendent
Examinations at Salina, New Cambria, Gypsum City, Assaria, Falun, Bavaria, and District No. 74 (in Glendale Twp.)
Reading and Penmanship: The Examination will be oral, and the Penmanship of Applicants will be graded from the manuscripts.

Grammar (Time, one hour)
1. Give nine rules for the use of Capital Letters.
2. Name the Parts of Speech and define those that have no modifications.
3. Define Verse, Stanza and Paragraph.
4. What are the Principal Parts of a verb? Give Principal Parts of do, lie, lay and run.
5. Define Case, Illustrate each Case.
6. What is Punctuation? Give rules for principal marks of Punctuation.
7. to 10. Write a composition of about 150 words and show therein that you understand the practical use of the rules of grammar.

Arithmetic (Time, 1.25 hours)

1. Name and define the Fundamental Rules of Arithmetic.
2. A wagon box is 2 ft. deep, 10 feet long, and 3 ft. wide. How many bushels of wheat will it hold?
3. If a load of wheat weighs 3942 lbs., what is it worth at 50 cts. bushel, deducting 1050 lbs. for tare?
4. District No. 33 has a valuation of $35,000. What is the necessary levy to carry on a school seven months at $50 per month, and have $104 for incidentals?
5. Find cost of 6720 lbs. coal at $6.00 per ton.
6. Find the interest of $512.60 for 8 months and 18 days at 7 percent.
7. What is the cost of 40 boards 12 inches wide and 16 ft. long at $20 per metre.
8. Find bank discount on $300 for 90 days (no grace) at 10 percent.
9. What is the cost of a square farm at $15 per acre, the distance around which is 640 rods?
10. Write a Bank Check, a Promissory Note, and a Receipt.

U.S. History (Time, 45 minutes)

1. Give the epochs into which U.S. History is divided.
2. Give an account of the discovery of America by Columbus.
3. Relate the causes and results of the Revolutionary War.
4. Show the territorial growth of the United States.
5. Tell what you can of the history of Kansas.

6. Describe three of the most prominent battles of the Rebellion.

7. Who were the following: Morse, Whitney, Fulton, Bell, Lincoln, Penn, and Howe?

8. Name events connected with the following dates: 1607, 1620, 1800, 1849, 1865.

Orthography (Time, one hour)

1. What is meant by the following: alphabet, phonetic, orthography, etymology, syllabication?

2. What are elementary sounds? How are they classified?

3. What are the following, and give examples of each: Trigraph subvocals, diphthong, cognate letters, linguals?

4. Give four substitutes for caret 'u.'

5. Give two rules for spelling words with final 'e.' Name two exceptions under each rule.

6. Give two uses of silent letters in spelling. Illustrate each.

7. Define the following prefixes and use in connection with a word: bi, dis, mis, pre, semi, post, non, inter, mono, sup. Mark diacritically and divide into syllables the following, and name the sign that indicates the sound: card, ball, mercy, sir, odd, cell, rise, blood, fare, last.

9. Use the following correctly in sentences: cite, site, sight, fane, fain, feign, vane, vain, vein, raze, raise, rays.

10. Write 10 words frequently mispronounced and indicate pronunciation by use of diacritical marks and by syllabication.

Geography (Time, one hour)

1. What is climate? Upon what does climate depend?
2. How do you account for the extremes of climate in Kansas?
3. Of what use are rivers? Of what use is the ocean?
4. Describe the mountains of North America.
5. Name and describe the following: Monrovia, Odessa, Denver, Manitoba, Hecla, Yukon, St. Helena, Juan Fernandez, Aspinwall, and Orinoco.
6. Name and locate the principal trade centers of the U.S.
7. Name all the republics of Europe and give capital of each.
8. Why is the Atlantic Coast colder than the Pacific in the same latitude?
9. Describe the process by which the water of the ocean returns to the sources of rivers.
10. Describe the movements of the earth. Give inclination of the earth.

A person who passed this exam, who had worked alongside his or her parents learning to take care of a home and a farm, might well be ready to be married at sixteen or seventeen. While this seems exceedingly young to us today, in the days when life expectancy was 46.3 years for men and 48.3 years for women, perhaps it wasn't so young after all.[28]

In any case, what seems apparent is that an individual's life trajectory was more fluid, more natural, and less artificially defined than it is today. A baby was born, grew up, and entered adulthood. Members of the family played the same games, listened to the same music, danced the same dances, read the same books.

In contrast, today we have a demographic defined and set apart as deserving greater independence and more sophisticated entertainment than children but without the full responsibility of adults. This started with the industrial revolution, followed by much-needed child-labor laws. As the twentieth century progressed, the push for more years of compulsory education led to district high schools, where children were bussed in from outlying rural locations to spend the greater part of their waking hours in each other's company, either on the bus or in the school building.

The term *teenager* was coined, and adolescence took on a life of its own. Music producers began focusing on this new special market. The 1955 classic movie *Rebel Without a Cause* began a trend of movies portraying teenage angst and rebellion against parents and society. All this cultural attention only served to more rigidly define and separate teenagers from mainstream society.

When you stop and think about it, it was very radical: Instead of identifying with their culture, teens were encouraged to identify with themselves, to judge themselves cool and set the standard by which everyone else's coolness would be measured.

And it was all exacerbated by the marketing geniuses who first glommed onto the idea that they could use this wedge—this artificial and unnecessary alienation—to sell their stuff.

We are reaping the whirlwind today. Far beyond hyper-consumerism, the forces of hyper-marketing make all of us oblivious to the steady erosion of what constitutes true freedom, as the following illustrates.

Choosy Beggars

Long ago, when I was a Washington, D.C., latchkey kid (before the term was coined), my mother would leave a few dollars and a list for me to go to the store after school. I'd walk a couple blocks down New Hampshire Avenue to the corner store, load a basket, cross my fingers that I'd have enough money and not have to put anything back, and then carry our bounty home in a double brown bag.

Fifty years later, I shop in a suburban mega-market fifty times the size of that humble shop. Between leaving my BMW (Big Mama Wagon) and returning to fill it with our family's food supply, I walk at least a mile, browsing aisles brimming with an assortment of food fit for a king: a dozen apple varieties, a hundred imported cheeses, meat and seafood, frozen foods galore, an astonishing assortment of breads, and an increasingly outrageous array of ice cream.

These days, grocery shopping is more of an art form than a survival tactic—each grocery cart a highly personal expression of all that we fancy ourselves to be.

But, oh, how much we've lost—even as we've gained.

It hit me the other morning. In a mustard-aisle meltdown, I nearly collapsed beneath the weight of all my choices. A multitude of specialty items...my cart in standby mode...my hand reaching, then hesitating... the labels becoming a blur. So many mustards, so little time.

A similar panic hit me that afternoon at the post office as I was trying to buy a hundred stamps.

The clerk offered me a vast selection from which to choose, including Love Ribbons, Heart Health, Aloha Shirts, Vanishing Species, Tiffany Lamps, and New Mexico Statehood.

"What about a roll of regular stamps?" I pleaded, trying to avert the mind-numbing selection process: Which stamp would send the right message to my editors? Which would be the perfect expression of me?

That evening I was in the throes of comparing cell-phone rates when my son, a high-school junior, brought me a catalog from which to order his design-your-own senior ring—twelve models, ten colors, five cuts of stones, and fifty possible side engravings. The selection took us an hour.

Overcome with nostalgia, I spent the rest of the evening searching for and finding my own high-school ring. The stone was blue, our official school color, the sides engraved with our high-school insignia and the year: 1965. That year my only choice was to order the boy's ring or the diminutive girl's version—in those days an easy decision.

I don't remember feeling shortchanged at all.

By contrast, today I feel ripped off, seeing how my most precious resource—time—is steadily stolen away with each meaningless decision I make. I remember with fondness the '50s grocery where I chose between white bread and brown, red apples and green, American and Swiss, dill and sweet. Only two mustards graced the shelf then: the regular yellow and its racy brown cousin. Today I grab the original like a lifeline, determined to negotiate the remaining aisles of this "Vanity Fair" with as much detachment as I can muster.

Now, with a few extra minutes to ponder the things that matter, I'm seeing that there's something even more maleficent than the moments we lose as our marketplace mushrooms. There's the deception by which our sense of freedom shifts from inalienable rights to economic choices, thus becoming largely an illusion based on which car you drive, detergent you use, jewelry you collect, or hamburger you eat. Have it your way.

The more options Americans have, the more our need for self-determination is sated by inconsequential choices like stamps and mustard and rings—the less fire we have for the freedoms our government continues to withhold (i.e., school vouchers) or begins to take away (i.e., religious expression).

In *Pilgrim's Progress* (OK, I know my evangelical roots are showing, but there's a point to be made here), John Bunyan notes that we cannot avoid Vanity Fair unless we leave this world. But we can pass through without getting caught up in the lust of the marketplace if, as his hero Christian says, we only buy the truth.

There is only one decision that really matters: "Choose this day whom you will serve" (Joshua 24:15). When I focus on that choice, the others fade in importance and I'm reminded that when it comes to options, less can really mean more.

If you are getting the impression that there is a war going on for the soul of your child, then you've heard me loud and clear. And yet, when faced with the Goliath of greed and determination to turn our kids into mindless consumers, would you give in? If you had only a slingshot, wouldn't you at least pick it up?

The truth is you *can* draw the line and defend it. As parents, our heavenly Father has given us all we need. It's just up to us to take a stand and teach our children to do the same.

Who Owns Your Child's Heart and Mind?

This is not just one of the struggles we face as parents. *It is the defining one*, the one we have to get right if we want everything else to fall into place. We must understand that in the spiritual realm a war is raging—a war in which we are constantly tempted by appeals to our senses. Its object is to make us slaves to a materialistic, anti-theistic world, a world where we each see ourselves as the center of the universe, entitled to find happiness or fulfillment in whatever product presents the most persuasive image, a world in which there is no moral compass, a world of moral relativism in which I decide what's right or wrong.

This is not a battle the Church can fight on our behalf while we keep our noses to the grindstone, perhaps even doing a great job of earning a living and keeping the home fires burning. In these times, with the sophistication of evil surrounding our children via the media and the mall, we have to do more than just show up with our kids at Sunday Mass and make sure they go to CCD classes. The bottom line is that our children's spiritual education is up to us—including how they apply what they hear at church and learn in CCD. If that is missing, nothing else matters.

During our twenty years of evangelicalism, our family sought out churches full of serious, committed believers with strong godly families. (One problem with evangelicalism is this kind of self-selection, as opposed to the parish system where the wheat and the tares are mixed—a biblical pattern that involves trusting God). The last evangelical church our family attended was the best ever—with home-schooling families galore, many birth control–free, and mega-vans pulling in on Sunday full of children carrying their own Bibles.

We didn't leave because we found anything wanting; we left because, as I described in chapter one God called us to Catholicism. While many of our children were already grown and have continued their evangelical journeys, those still at home went to Mass with us because the way we raised them had led them to trust us no matter what.

True story: Sometimes that trust was put to the test. I will never forget fifteen-year-old Maddy's first Mass. As she watched the Communion processional, her eyes got as big as saucers and she looked at me with disbelief.

"Mom, I go to school with these kids and I didn't even know they were Christians. Some of them are the worst kids in the school."

This was a hard one for me to explain: that people can be exposed to the truth and beauty that is the Catholic Church and just not get it. That unlike the very conservative evangelicals we'd been associated with—and Maddy's Mormon friends whose beliefs were heresy but whose daily conduct was exemplary—the Catholic Church respects individual free will without a cult-like system of oversight. It's ironic, since most people think of the Church as rigid. While God's truth is unchanging and eternal and our church has a God-given hierarchy, how we respond is up to each individual.

Evidently these young people had failed to connect the dots—which is why even then I began to hope that someday God would help me in communicating the importance of Catholic parents in the spiritual growth and commitment of their children. If faith isn't nurtured at home, it will wither, and sometimes even die.

Faced with this responsibility of raising God-first children in a me-first world, what is a parent to do?

Preparing for Battle

The battle may look complex, but it is simple:

> No one can serve two masters; for either he will hate the one and love the other, or he will be devoted to the one and despise the other.
> You cannot serve God and mammon.
> —Matthew 6:24

While our first instinct may be to handle the problem through rules and restrictions, this is not the best way to go. While we can control what our children see and hear in the media during their early years, there will come a time when things become more complicated and situations arise outside of our control—visits to friends and neighbors, or even relatives with different values, for instance.

And honestly, imposing control from the outside is not a good plan anyway. What you want to do is win your child's heart. Rather than being forced to accept what may appear to be arbitrary restrictions, you want your children to understand why some things are sinful or dangerous, even when they don't appear so. You want to equip them to make good choices when they are grown up, so they can resist the temptation to indulge in entertainment that cloaks challenges to their values in an irresistible package. You want them to develop discernment and then to have the strength and courage to use it well.

God knew that, in all times and all places, his followers would face this kind of spiritual battle. Ours look different, and today's parents need sophisticated strategies to defend their precious progeny against the constant efforts of the Enemy to neutralize their faith and make it meaningless and ineffective—so Sunday's Mass often is muddled with memories of craziness the night before—but our weapons were described and handed down to us as the Church was being born:

> Finally, be strong in the Lord and in the strength of his might. Put on the whole armor of God, that you may be able to stand against the wiles of the devil. For we are not contending against flesh and blood, but against the principalities, against the powers, against the world rulers of this present darkness, against the spiritual hosts of wickedness in the heavenly places. Therefore take the whole armor of God, that you may be able to withstand in the evil day, and having done all, to stand. Stand therefore, having girded your loins with truth, and having put on the breastplate of righteousness, and having shod your feet with the equipment of the gospel of peace; besides all these, taking the shield of faith, with which you can quench all the flaming darts of the evil one. And take

the helmet of salvation, and the sword of the Spirit, which is the word of God. Pray at all times in the Spirit, with all prayer and supplication. To that end keep alert with all perseverance, making supplication for all the saints. (Ephesians 6:10–18)

Time Is on Our Side

Even the most conscientious parents—working hard to earn a living, keep a home, and maintain a secure future for their children—will be the first to admit that the hardest resource for them to give is time. However, after forty-three years of mothering, I am absolutely convinced that the language of time is the language of love. Forget *quality time* vs. *quantity time*—every child needs both.

Some families have factors in their lives they just can't change. But there are changes any family—no matter the circumstances—can change to create more quality *and* quantity time:

- Limit TV and gaming time.
- Watch one or two worthwhile TV shows a week with your kids and take the time to talk about them, particularly discussing what they reveal about character.
- Read aloud—our kids loved listening to their dad read anything Dickens, also *The Chronicles of Narnia,* and *The Lord of the Rings* (see "Story Power").
- Work on jigsaw puzzles together; having a puzzle going on creates opportunities for different mini-groups within the family to sit and chat while accomplishing something together
- Cards and board games: old-fashioned? Yes. Boring? No.
- Rock Band? Guitar Hero? These have taken the corniness out of karaoke and are fun for the whole family.

- If you're busy in the evening, let your kids know they may interrupt you—politely. Your work can wait, but whatever your child wants to say may not. Make eye contact and listen. You never know what you might hear.
- Tuck them in, no matter how old they are.

A Simple Recipe for Success

Want to maximize your children's chance for success? Boost their grades and SAT scores, develop good self-esteem and social skills, plus help them avoid cigarettes, drugs, and alcohol?

Just thirty minutes a day is all it takes. You never have to leave home or spend a dime. Yet study after study concludes that one simple practice can make these parental dreams come true.

All you have to do is sit down to a family dinner.

These days, that may be easier said than done, which is probably why we've seen a 33 percent decrease in the last thirty years in families who say they have dinner together regularly. Think about it: In 1970, kids played after school pretty much on their own—roller skating, holding impromptu backyard baseball games, Barbie soap operas, or just plain hanging out—while Mom made dinner. Dad came home, Mom called the kids, and voila: the family dinner.

Today's families are different; many have two breadwinners or single parents. But even in a traditional family like mine, dealing with a heap of homework and a gazillion extracurricular activities adds a crazy spin to the concept of dinner. Not to mention countless hours of parental Behind the Wheel. So who has time to cook?

Still, those studies are hard to ignore. Family dinners mean kids with better eating habits and good manners and social graces—kids who know how to make dinner conversation and who will be welcome and confident wherever they go. And—on a more serious note—kids with a decreased chance of teen pregnancy or suicide.

And by the way, as a former single mother, I know it's not easy to sit down and eat together, but since kids from single-parent families are most at risk, they need family dinners more than anyone.

So how does a busy family do it? Here are a few suggestions:

1. Keep dinnertime flexible. On nights Zach had karate, we had dinner at 5:00. On nights when Ben had after-school rehearsal, we had it at 7:00. I look for a window of opportunity when, even if we can't all be home, at least most of us will be. But make sure to provide snacks when dinner will be late to keep crankiness at bay.

2. Use a crock-pot. First thing in the morning, throw in some meat, mushroom soup, and Lipton onion soup mix—or try spaghetti sauce with defrosted frozen meatballs.

3. Stretch these moments of togetherness by involving your children in meal prep. Instead of finding peace by scooting the kids out of the kitchen, make them feel welcome and necessary. Even the smallest can stand on a stool and watch the action.

4. Turn off the TV. Don't answer the phone.

5. Keep things simple. Once a week we do Breakfast Night: pancakes, sausage, and eggs.

6. Have some conversation starters (such as a Bible verse, some song lyrics, a bit of American history) and encourage everyone to participate. In the words of Ronald Reagan, "All great change in America begins at the dinner table."[29]

Instead of a rotating chore, make cleanup fun by working together—as the saying goes, "Many hands make light work." Try singing songs like "A Spoonful of Sugar" or "Just Whistle While You Work." If you're having a good time, your kids will too.

No matter how simple the meal, a few candles will lift it to another level. And don't forget to say grace—with feeling. As the Bible says, "Train up a child in the way he should go, and when he is old he will not depart from it" (Proverbs 22:6).

One more thing: making dinnertime a priority—putting your own special motherhood energy into each meal—offers rewards when your children are grown and gone. Filled with warm memories of special moments around the family table, they will rarely turn down an invitation for a family dinner. That's the kind of bond that can only be established when they are growing up.

Sit down, relax, and get to know each other better. The bottom line is this: Kids don't care if it's fish sticks and French fries, as long as time with you is on the menu. That's what they'll always remember.

Bottom line: Your surest weapon in the battle against consumerist forces is the bond of love and trust you have with your child. You can only build this through time and availability. Whatever you have to trade to make this happen—less overtime, fewer social engagements, even fewer commitments to church activities—is worth it.

Raising your children is one place where you want to hear God say in the end: "Well done, my good and faithful servant." He won't be saying that about how much money you earned or how clean you kept your house, or how many bake sales you were a part of. The main thing is that we are stewards of our children—*his* children—and the potential they hold for the future.

With Open Hearts, We Can Open Minds

When your children are secure in your love and you're secure in their trust, you have a perfect teaching situation. While homeschooling parents are used to thinking of themselves as teachers, sometimes parents who have delegated their children's academic education to others (and there's nothing wrong with that) lose sight of the fact that no matter what, they are still their children's most important teacher.

Don't ever forget that. We are not just the caretakers of our children's material needs; we are the ones who monitor what our children are taking in wherever they go, who bless what they're learning or explain to them why it's not worthy of blessing. In today's anti-theistic climate, it's important that we monitor what is going on in our children's classrooms and discuss it with them.

One of the most important lessons we need to pass on to our kids is an awareness of the media swamp surrounding us. As I mentioned, even if you limit TV viewing or don't even have a TV, their friends do and they are learning all the jargon, the attitudes, and what makes a kid cool.

Kids need to discern when they are being exploited. They need to develop self-awareness and recognize where they are vulnerable. You can teach your children to pick apart ads and analyze what is going on and what strings are being pulled. You can let them know that they are more than the faceless consumers the media assume them to be. They need to understand why teens are targets—not only for the dollars they spend now, thinking who they are is reflected in whether they drink Coke or Pepsi, eat at McDonalds or Burger King, dress in American Eagle or Abercrombie and Fitch—but also because these companies want to capture their loyalty so they can have the best shot of keeping them on board all their lives.

Is Your Body a Billboard?
Remember the good old days when being appropriately dressed meant making sure your labels were tucked inside your clothes? What a brilliant strategy it was when clothing manufacturers persuaded consumers there was status to be found in prominently displaying the name of the manufacturer—sometimes in six-inch letters on T-shirts and sweatshirts—thus reinforcing the self-concept of the brand-identified wearer even while providing free advertising space!

When I asked young people via email how they dealt with consumerism, I was pleased to find that some were already aware and had strategies to resist:

Kristen: "There is a lot of pressure in teenage culture to have the right things, especially with regards to clothing and electronics. Sometimes I felt so left out just because I wasn't wearing the right brand jeans, even though I knew my jeans cost half as much and would last twice as long as theirs. I made it a policy not to shop at the 'popular' stores like Abercrombie & Fitch and Hollister, because I didn't want to waste my money in pursuit of superficial popularity, nor did I want to support these companies and their blatantly sexual advertising. I feel that I have less than others sometimes, especially at my private college where many students own BMWs and fly home regularly, but it doesn't bother me anymore. I don't want more stuff. My parents didn't buy me the popular items, and I wasn't spoiled, but I never went too long without something I sincerely wanted. I think the key to Biblical consumerism is to examine your motives for buying and see if they align with God's Word. Also, it is good to wait a while before buying something, especially if you're an impulse buyer like I am."

Matt, public-school graduate, currently a freshman at University of Missouri at Kansas City: "There is a lot of pressure to have certain things, and I was influenced by that early on in junior high and the beginning of high school. I think once I really embraced the Scripture in Matthew 6:21, 'For where your treasure is, there will your heart be also,' I realized that it wasn't that important to have a bunch of useless stuff; so much of it was fads. I don't really feel I have less than others (although maybe I do in the sense of materialism), but I just try and appreciate the things I do have, and not take them for granted."

Alyse: "I must say that I do not have much trouble at all on how many 'things' I have and how many 'things' other people have. To be honest with you, I do not understand why so many people feel they have to have the same things other people have and look the same way other people look. When I look at society, I am saddened. It seems to me like all the teenagers have to (or at least try to) look like all the other teenagers. All the stars have to look like all the other stars; all the singers have to look like all the other singers. I feel you need to be who God made you to be."

Brett: "Having *things* in the teenage life does mean a little. Though some say it doesn't affect them, it does. But as you see in many other countries, people who have a lot less than us are much happier. I think those who want more are fooling themselves. Those who have a lot still think they need more, making it a never-ending circle that will cause destruction. But as Christians we are not of the earthly world and as hard as it is, we should care nothing about earthly possessions. My parents did something really helpful. First, they showed me how happy mission trips to the less fortunate are by earthly standards. They also didn't give me everything I wanted."

Parents can start resisting consumerism in their children's lives by blocking consumerist channels. They can sit down and watch their teens' favorite shows with them to see what's really going on.

Parents can teach kids about product placement, a concept that really took off in 1982 when the movie *E.T.* portrayed a cute little kid luring an irresistible little alien through a wooded area to his bedroom with a trail of Reese's Pieces. Within two weeks of *E.T.'s* release, sales for the obscure candy shot through the roof.

Now it's a rare film that doesn't add cash to its coffers with product placement contracts for everything from Huggies diapers to Starbucks coffee to DeLorean dream cars. Rates are structured depending on how the product appears. A can of Coke sitting on a table might cost the Coca-Cola company a certain amount, but if Tom Cruise picks it up and opens it, it costs a whole lot more. And if he actually brings it to his lips—well, you can imagine!

The more our kids know about the inner workings of the advertising world, the less susceptible they will be to such subliminal manipulation—and the more available their minds will be to God and the things that really matter.

> **Understanding Teen Marketing: Resources for Parents**
> **The Merchants of Cool**
> http://www.pbs.org/wgbh/pages/frontline/shows/cool/
> *An online PBS report on the creators and marketers of popular culture for teenagers*
>
> **Media Smarts**
> http://mediasmarts.ca/tags/64
> *A Canadian site that helps parents and teachers equip kids with critical thinking skills in order to understand how the media works and how to make intelligent decisions*

Here's a thoughtful topic for family discussion: When it comes to TV, what is the product being sold? Who is the customer?

As they watch TV, your kids probably think of themselves as the customers, with the ads they watch displaying a parade of products being sold. Not so! For television networks, the real customers they serve are their advertisers. And the viewers—including your children—are the product being sold.

That's why the cost for a commercial can vary from nineteen dollars for a thirty-second daytime spot on a local cable channel to four million dollars for the same amount of time during the Super Bowl, which attracts the largest television audience every year. The price paid by the customer/advertiser is based on the number of viewers during that time slot—the same way we buy meat by the pound.

Encourage your kids to look at commercials with a critical eye, identifying what factors underlie the message: guilt, greed, manipulation, fear, flattery, status-seeking, and so on.

And one final thought: Children cannot learn to control their impulses for more, more, more if we say yes, yes, yes. Even if you had the money to buy your child everything he wants, it's really not the loving thing to do. Parents must be good role models; you must learn to say no.

CHAPTER SIX

Purity, Principles, and Priorities

"I think I found a boy."

Sophia's voice on the phone was a mixture of many things—her signature little-girl Marilyn Monroe-ish breathiness, a quiet confidence, and a sense of standing at the brink of a promise fulfilled. Her words were based on an early reader beloved in our family: *The Puppy Who Found a Boy*. I knew exactly what she meant, and somehow I knew that her future had just changed forever, thanks to her patience in trusting God.

At twenty, having bypassed the high-school dating scene (always believing there was something better ahead), Sophia was entering her first relationship.

She was a sophomore at Liberty University, founded by evangelical Jerry Falwell. (When Tripp and I converted to Catholicism, we had three children at Liberty, and as *I Love Lucy*'s Ricky Ricardo would say, they had a lot of 'splainin' to do about their wayward parents!) At the time, Sophia was a talented young woman equipping herself for a career in music and children's theater, but she was the first to admit that what she wanted more than anything was to one day be a wife and mother.

His name was Joshua (and yes, it does cause family confusion when a son or daughter brings home someone with the same name as a sibling—but not enough to send him packing), and he had been raised in a similar Christian family, right down to *Veggie Tales* and *Sleep Sound in Jesus*. He was also a music major at Liberty and shared a townhouse with Sophia's brothers—right next door to the one she shared with her friends. Sophia and Josh had shared a lengthy friendship centered on bicycling, hiking, and (of course) singing before discovering that God might have more in mind.

Things were a little complicated because his family lived in a different state, but we got to meet Josh for the first time at a family vacation in Nags Head, North Carolina. He fit in as though he'd been with us forever. We loved him immediately. And we felt he was an answer to the prayers Tripp had begun every night over Sophia's cradle when she was a baby: that God would lead her to the perfect husband, that even as we were raising her to be pure, to be equipped to be a godly wife and mother, another set of parents somewhere out there were praying the same prayer for their son.

Though Sophia had been homeschooled when we lived in California, she had entered public school when we settled in Virginia in 2002. It was not an easy transition for an introvert who'd just moved cross-country. We had many conversations in which Sophia tearfully begged me to homeschool her, but intuitively—and when I say intuitively, I mean according to how I perceive the Holy Spirit leading me—I felt she was exactly where she needed to be. The decisions parents are called to make, especially when the still, small voice directs us to do something contrary to what other Christian/Catholic parents would do, can be very, very difficult. When we moved to Virginia, I expected to continue homeschooling and to teach at homeschool conferences. Ironically, in moving to what Evangelicals consider the homeschool capital of the world—Purcellville, Virginia—I felt led to put my kids in public school. Only time would reveal whether I was really hearing correctly and being obedient—and obedience often involves a leap of faith.

Ten years later, I am convinced it was indeed the right path for our family, and I've also learned not to judge other parents. What looks like a tangent may have something to do with what God wants to accomplish. We can't begin to know his reasons—we are simply called to obey.

And so, despite the pulls on my heartstrings—and my own tears—I kept Sophia in school, trying to encourage her and soften the transition as best I could. In the end, she blossomed in ways she never would have as an introvert unchallenged in a comfortable homeschool setting. In public school, she was exposed to many teachers who found her to be a dream student—intelligent, attentive, thoughtful, analytical—and whose specific praise built her confidence in a way her parents could not have. She had outlets for music and drama that allowed her to develop her gifts, gifts that would help balance her introversion. She learned to choose friends who shared the same values as she did, who dressed and behaved modestly but who also had wild and crazy wholesome fun. They went out in mixed guys-and-mostly-girls groups to the movies, picnics, and even school dances, where they carved out a space far from the sketchy freak dancing and just had a good time without the pressure of sex and all the problems and clouded vision that entails.

Sophia was our eighth child. While she was our third daughter, she was the first one born to Tripp and me, as Samantha and Jasmine were fourteen and seven when we married. She enjoyed a spiritual head start with two well-seasoned parents, highly motivated to do their best. She also had the advantage of four older brothers who'd been steeped in the ethic of purity, three who embraced it for themselves and one who chose otherwise—all real world lessons backing up the truth of what their parents had taught.

By the way, let me take this opportunity to say that, for purposeful parents, it is much easier to keep your children on the straight and narrow when you have a big family. When so much of what you teach and ask them to honor goes against the flow of the modern world, a big family provides a bastion of acceptance, affirmation, and security.

In a way, Sophia is the perfect example of what can happen when you work to give your children a good start. This is not to say that if you work hard you can expect all your children to turn out perfectly; since God did not create us from a cookie cutter and gave us free will, parenthood is not as simple as following a recipe and expecting a certain outcome.

But I'm borrowing Sophia's story because it illustrates

- The power of obedience and how God rewards it
- The generational enhancement of those rewards
- God's mercy in forgiving parents their sins and allowing them to share in building a beautiful family on his foundation

Tripp and I were raised in fatherless homes with mothers distracted by their own desperate situations. We had no religion, no values, no moral compass. As a result, at the ages of twenty-eight (Tripp) and thirty-five (me), we entered marriage with a lot of baggage. The one advantage we had going for us was that we knew the freedom we had chased was an illusion, and we recognized that sexual freedom was actually slavery. We were completely dedicated to raising children who would be emotionally healthy and secure in the love of their family, who would grow into adults with more wisdom and stability than their parents. For the first few years, we were running on our own steam and our good intentions were manifested in material comforts. But after our spiritual seeking led us to a born-again experience, from that point on, whenever we faced issues or questions concerning our children, we did not face them alone, but with the power of the Holy Spirit to nudge us toward the light and to steer us away from danger whenever we missed a step.

My oldest daughter, Samantha, was seventeen and a senior in high school when this happened. She'd been dating her sweetheart, Kip—whom she'd known since fifth grade—for a couple of years. During that time, she'd had no spiritual guidance or from me or anyone else, so I wasn't surprised when I found out she and Kip were having sex. What did surprise me was what came out of my mouth:

"Well, Samantha, God forgives you and so do I."

Hearing those words of grace, Samantha burst into tears. "Mom, I know in my heart it's wrong and we try to stop, but we'll go a few weeks and then we can't help ourselves," she sobbed.

"That's because you don't have God in your life," I heard myself say wisely, although I really had no wisdom at all at that point, just the Holy Spirit answering a distress call on behalf of a newbie Christian parent.

The next day, which happened to be Father's Day, Tripp called Kip (who didn't have a clue what had happened) and asked him to come to his office. He walked him through some verses in the Bible he'd found the night before, and then explained to him—man-to-man—that Samantha would never trust him, never know for sure that he loved her for who she was and not for what she put out, unless he agreed to put sex aside until they were married.

As a result of these two encounters, Samantha and Kip became Christians too. Though it was difficult, they established boundaries for themselves and maintained a pure relationship for two years. They married at nineteen, over the objections of many people who didn't understand that they had shown through their obedience a level of maturity and commitment to their relationship that many of their elders never reach. It's amazing how prejudiced even some Christians are against early marriage, even though we of all people should understand that God's plan for some couples may be to marry young.

Now married for twenty-three years, Samantha and Kip have six children—five by birth and one through adoption. They are committed Christians, homeschooling and active in their community. They regret not getting off to a perfect start, but because God got hold of their lives earlier than he got hold of Tripp's and mine, they entered their marriage with much less baggage, along with the joy of knowing that when it came to sexual intimacy, they had only known each other.

My second daughter Jasmine, who was eleven when Tripp and I became Christians, had a born-again experience soon after at the first church we attended, and she has never wavered in her faith. She was twenty-one when she met her husband, and they were engaged and married within a year. He was the first man she ever kissed, and she waited until their wedding night to give herself to him completely. Today they are a strong Christian homeschooling family with seven children.

Samantha and Jasmine may have gotten off to a rocky start, but through God's grace and their cooperation in their own redemption, God was able to build something wonderful in each of their lives.

God also gave us a chance to see what happens when parents partner with him from the beginning. Our boys—Joshua, Matthew, and Benjamin—were four-and a-half, three, and eighteen months when Tripp and I began our journey as Christian parents. Zachary was born the following year. Sophia was born in 1989, Jonathan (who has Down syndrome) in 1992, and Madeleine in 1993. Since then we've adopted three baby boys with Down syndrome.

With this set of children, we were given the grace of time as we started from scratch to create a godly plan for bringing up our children with a healthy and respectful attitude toward sex. We listened to Christian parenting shows on the radio and read every Christian parenting book we could get our hands on. Since we were not Catholics, we did not have access to a fully formed theology to provide the basis of what we would teach, but our plans for teaching our children about sex and the family would be affirmed twenty years later when we discovered Pope John Paul II's teaching on the Theology of the Body. The uncompromised and unchanging doctrine and wisdom of the Church gives Catholic parents a head start—as long as they decide to use it!

While Tripp and I didn't have the advantage of being Catholic initially, I believe God rewarded our sincerity (and I believe that part of his plan for our family involved our eventually becoming Catholic) and helped us through the Holy Spirit to find the right answers to our questions. Because of this, there was nothing haphazard about how we taught our family about sex.

First of all, we understood intuitively that sex is not something that stands on its own, but is spiritually tied in with God's plan for the family. The concept of purity we want for our children isn't a *turning away from sex*, but a *turning towards God*. It isn't like Just Say No to Drugs. Drugs are bad for you, and so we say no. Sex is good—a wonderful gift from God—so we don't say no, we say, "Wait. Wait until your wedding night."

Sex in a Nutshell

In today's world, where sex is cheap and easy to come by, we can help our kids by giving them a vision of what sex is really all about and how valuable it is. Here's what Tripp and I try to pass on to our children:

Just as every car has an owner's manual to help us understand and keep it running at its best, the Bible is God's owner's manual for his creation. Things go best for us when we follow what God says.

God's plan is one husband, one wife—with no sex outside this sacred union.

It's not really so much about sex being *forbidden*, but about it being *reserved* so that it can fulfill his plan for marriage. That's because sex is such an incredibly wonderful experience that when a husband and wife have their first sex together, they are bound together more securely.

It's the exquisite richness of this experience that makes it worth waiting for. So as you grow up, even though your body may send signals that it's ready for sex and even though you may want it, you choose to wait in order to make that moment in your marriage as special as it was meant to be.

God will help you if you ask him.

And just to prove that God's plan for his children is always best, studies confirm that those with the most satisfying sex lives are not the sexual adventurers, but the couples who wait for marriage:

Couples who wait until marriage are happier with the quality of sex than couples who have intercourse before their vows.

What's more, couples who delay sex until their wedding night have more stable and happier marriages than couples who have premarital sex, according to the study, which appears in the *Journal of Family Psychology.*

The study involved 2,035 married participants in an online assessment of marriage called "RELATE." According to the study, people who waited until marriage:

- rated sexual quality 15 percent higher than people who had premarital sex
- rated relationship stability as 22 percent higher
- rated satisfaction with their relationships 20 percent higher

The benefits were about half as strong for couples who became sexually active later in their relationships but before marriage.[30]

Teaching our children about sex must be in the context of trusting God, and trusting their parents to tell them the truth. More than being given a set of arbitrary rules, they need to understand how the boundaries their parents set—based on those God has given us—work together to guide them toward a more promising future.

We've Come a Long Way, Baby—or Have We?

I remember a classmate named Peggy in high school. By far the cutest and peppiest cheerleader, she had everything the rest of us girls wanted, including the captain of the football team. I was nerd enough to feel special when Peggy nudged me during history class to slide my paper a little left so she could copy my answers. That was about as close to the popular crowd as I ever got.

In our senior year, Peggy suddenly disappeared with no warning or explanation. You could almost feel the hush around her empty desk. After a time, the whispers began—whispers that the most popular girl in our class was pregnant and that her parents had shipped her off somewhere to have the baby. We never saw her again.

Back in the '60s we were innocent. My friends and I couldn't begin to grasp the idea of someone our age having a baby. We couldn't even begin to grasp the idea that Peggy had had sex. Was it possible that maybe she'd gotten pregnant just from making out?

Those were the days! And while I'm not suggesting that they were perfect or that the problem of teenage pregnancy didn't exist, I am invoking the past for a moment to make a point: Parents today have to work much harder to help their kids avoid making mistakes than parents of previous generations.

Through movies, music, and the mall—and in their high-school classes—today's kids have been fed a steady diet of moral relativism: the idea that there are no moral absolutes, and that the worst sin is to judge someone else. In this age of enlightenment, a girl like Peggy doesn't have to disappear. Instead, she can remain in school with only a short break to have the baby. She might even be voted homecoming queen on her return, as was one teen mother in a small town in New York recently.

No scandal, no guilt, no shame.

Today the importance of waiting until marriage for sex, waiting until marriage to live together, and waiting until marriage to have babies has been marginalized as the quaint views of the religious fringe. Christian parents no longer have society on their side when it comes to helping kids navigate the rapids of the teen years.

While songs like yesteryear's "When I Fall in Love" or "Goin' to the Chapel" helped reinforce the romantic aspect of boy/girl relationships, they also defined the limits and the goals. It's a clear example of how single-minded our culture was back in the *Father Knows Best* and *Leave*

It to Beaver days. This is no longer true for today's generation.

Moral corruption has occurred with today's song lyrics, as well as with TV and movies. What would have once been considered pornography is now available for the price of admission or the click of a remote. During my teenage years a movie called *Splendor in the Grass* starring Natalie Wood and Warren Beatty was groundbreaking in its portrayal of teen sex (in keeping with the times, the sex was suggested but not shown). Nevertheless, at the end of the movie, the emphasis was on the great unhappiness that resulted from breaking social taboos.

The switch from romance to eroticism in entertainment has put enormous pressure on today's teens. But it's even more pervasive and subtle than the soft porn now passing for R-rated in movie theaters.

From their youngest years, today's kids have grown up in a culture increasingly obsessed with sex, where the vividly detailed sex lives of national leaders are delivered with the daily news, and where Victoria's Secret and Herbal Essence commercials assault our visual and auditory senses during prime-time TV. Pornography is a mouse-click away. And young readers can try their emerging word analysis skills in the grocery checkout line with *Cosmopolitan*, asking, "What's an or-ga-zim, Mommy?"

Even the most permissive parents would never have dreamed of letting their daughters dress in a sexually provocative way. And their daughters couldn't have found such clothing in kid sizes anyway. Now any ten-year-old who wants to can dress like a call girl, and today's parents have a difficult task helping their daughters find clothing that doesn't send the wrong message.

This means that in addition to setting clear limits, you need to equip your teens to avoid temptation.

You may need to rethink dating, because dating for two kids who grew up in the sixties listening to the Shirelles is different than dating for two kids who grew up in the eighties listening to Bon Jovi. And dating is different for today's kids, who've been indoctrinated through the media and sometimes the school with the idea that sex is great and why not go for it.

No matter what generation we're talking about, the thing all three couples have in common is their hormones. God chose to make the sexual urge a powerful one, all the better to bond a husband and wife in marriage. Every teen has to deal with that reality.

But a couple in the fifties had the backing of their families, schools, churches, and communities to help them draw the line and hold it. They might spend some time alone in a car and kiss or make out, but there was a powerful taboo against going all the way.

A couple in the eighties had it a little bit tougher, since during this time of social transition, they received competing messages from the culture.

But for today's teen couples in our sex-saturated society where virginity is openly scorned, the combination of hormones and license makes temptation a much more formidable reality.

Though there are other temptations, it is in the area of maintaining their purity that our children need the most support. If our culture were as consistent and adamant about the dangers of teen sex—and not just physical, but psychological and emotional—as it is about the dangers of cigarettes, drugs, and alcohol, parents might be able to relax a little.

But it's not and we can't.

Say you've taken a proactive approach with your teens regarding purity, and you're sure they're committed to waiting until marriage. Setting limits is just the beginning. Now you need to equip them to avoid temptation.

Here are some ideas that work:

Postpone dating for as long as possible. By sixth and seventh grade, some kids are dating. But no matter how many parents are supporting their kids in these budding relationships, and no matter how cute and innocent they seem, it is wise to discourage them.

The sixth-grade son of a friend of mine told his mom that three girls liked him and were demanding that he choose one to go with. When he told his mom one had pressured him to meet him at the movies, she simply said, "Son, I don't think you need to be thinking about that right now."

"You're right, Mom," he said, looking relieved.

The precociousness of today's tween girls can be pretty scary. As my four sons hit the teen years, I was shocked by how aggressive girls had become, and I found this to be a constant complaint among moms. Girls have always matured faster than boys, but in the past twenty years, the gap has accelerated rapidly. In addition to the stripping away of a girl's natural modesty and her earlier sexualization, more and more girls are growing up fatherless and desperately seeking male affirmation that only a dad can safely fulfill. Many girls are very pushy about nailing down relationships, calling boys, and going public as a couple. We have advised our daughters not to go that route. We have advised our sons to stay away from girls who do.

The truth is, there is so much more developmentally that should be going on with kids this age—like finding one's way around in a larger and more densely populated school, figuring out how to deal with five or six teachers with different personalities, building good study habits, bonding with friends, developing compassion, not to mention building a relationship with God. Although there is an increasing interest in the opposite sex, focusing too much energy on it can sidetrack a tween from some of the more important work that needs to be going on.

Then there is the cold hard fact I cited previously: Early dating leads to earlier sex. Period.

Support friendships with kids from like-minded families. My kids have all confirmed that the middle-school years represent a fork in the road; it's during those years that many kids decide which path they're going to take—whether they'll stick with their faith and family values, or whether they'll go their own way.

My kids managed to make it through those years by building friendships with friends with similar values—including Mormons, whose theology may be deeply flawed, but who my kids were quick to point out were, as a group, the most modest and pure students at school, which meant comfortable and supportive friendships for my girls, who were not even allowed to wear spaghetti straps.

Attending weekly Bible studies helped broaden my kids' base of like-minded friends. Though the popular crowd was dating, one way or another, my kids found friends content to wait but committed to having fun. They avoided parties they knew would involve drinking.

Encourage group dates. Okay, I'm not living in la-la land. Even as we discuss ways to help your teen keep his life balanced, teens need time with members of the opposite sex to learn how to feel comfortable and be friends. The reality is that they will develop crushes on each other. Any adult knows this is true because we did it ourselves.

Often, someone's crush will generate a group date. A bunch of kids will go to the movies or bowling or out to eat. Though there may be some undercurrent of who likes whom, a group date is a very safe way to give your teen some significant social time without the risks of one-on-one dating.

Be hospitable. Let your home be known as a great place for teens to hang out. Simply put, when your kids invite their friends to your house, you know what's going on. That's worth any extra work you may put in.

For some years, we had a breakfast night each week, with Dad in charge of serving pancakes, eggs, bacon, sausage, and orange juice. Since many families are too busy to eat big breakfasts these days, and because of the novelty of breakfast food after dark, kids loved to come over for this. I've also heard of families having taco nights or pizza nights.

Seeing your kids' friends on a regular basis is a great way to really get to know them. And someday that might make a difference in their lives.

Give your teen a cell phone. Cell phones are an essential part of today's parenting. Your kids should know that they can reach you at any time. And you need to know that you can reach them.

Shop for the best family plan. Be sure to share with your teen how the billing works, what your limits are, the fact that text messaging costs more, etc.

I remind my kids to take their cell phones when they leave, to turn them off during movies, but to turn them back on afterwards to check for messages.

Keep your teen accountable for destinations and timetables. In our family, we are all accountable for where we are to other members of the family. My kids need to know where Tripp and I are, and we need to know where they are.

When they are going to a party, I call to make sure the parents will be home. I give my kids a curfew—although the state of Virginia makes it easy because drivers under eighteen can't drive after midnight. My kids also know that if they leave one place for another, they must call home. This is where, for parents at least, cell phones are a gift from God.

Limit time alone with a member of the opposite sex. Our rule is that our kids cannot go into someone's house unless the parents are home. They can't have someone over unless their dad and I are home. As they've gotten older, we've made exceptions for friends of the same sex, but never the opposite.

Their bedrooms are off-limits to the opposite sex.

Cars can be risky territory, as anyone who has ever been a teenager knows. When our teens went out on dates alone at sixteen or seventeen (not all waited until college—no cookie-cutter kids, remember?), Tripp and I reminded them to limit their time in the car to getting where they need to go and back again.

Eliminate latchkey hours. As I've mentioned, I was a latchkey kid. And I'm sorry to say that, during the early eighties, my own two daughters were latchkey kids as well. Looking back, I regret that I ever put them in harm's way.

Today, there are approximately seven million latchkey kids in the U.S. All are greatly at risk. Research shows them more likely to skip school, make lower grades, have sex, get into trouble, and abuse drugs than those coming home to some kind of supervision or to an after-school program.

While many moms plan to stay home during the preschool years, thinking it's okay to work when the kids are older, the truth is a mother's continued presence in the home—at least during after school hours—can be of enormous benefit to her children.

If it's necessary for your family that both parents work, try to avoid your child coming home to an empty house. Talk to your employer about staggering your hours; perhaps one parent can start work earlier and come home earlier. Or you might find other parents in a similar situation and team up to provide supervision by forming a coop, with one parent taking off one afternoon each week, or pooling resources to hire supervision for your group.

The goal is to provide the best possible safety and security for your children.

Monitor entertainment. A recent study found that teens who watch sexually-oriented TV shows are more likely to engage in sex themselves, even if the TV content consists only of innuendo. *USA Today* reported on the study by psychologist Rebecca Collins, which was reported in the online journal *Pediatrics.*

> Kids who said they watched more sex-oriented programs at the beginning of the year were more likely than others their age to become sexually active during the next year. Those in the top 10% for viewing of sexually related scenes were twice as likely to engage in intercourse as those in the lowest 10%, Collins says. The more sex-oriented scenes they saw, the more likely they were to become sexually active.
>
> "It's social learning: 'monkey see, monkey do,'" Collins says. "If everyone's talking about sex or having it, and something bad hardly ever comes out of it, because it doesn't on TV, then they think, 'Hey, the whole world's doing it, and I need to.'"[31]

Safeguard computers. Involvement in online pornography can happen in the very best of families. I know, because it happened in mine.

Looking for a site I'd visited the day before, I was scrolling through my history and stumbled onto the names of several sites I wouldn't have visited in a million years. I clicked on one and was shocked at what I saw.

Now, here I was with four teenage sons—and a husband to boot. I gathered them all up and told them what I'd found. No one admitted to using my computer to visit porn sites. But finally, through checking times we knew it had to be one particular individual. Confronted with the evidence, he first denied it and then confessed, but said it was the first time it had happened and would never happen again.

Why didn't I have any filters in place? Because I'd homeschooled my sons, they hadn't had a lot of exposure to worldly stuff, and they were such good boys that I hadn't realized the urgency of the situation.

I was wrong.

For one thing, as a woman, I had no idea how vulnerable all men— even the nicest—are to pornography. One of my biggest regrets is that this blind spot led me to overlook an area where I could have helped the men in my life avoid temptation.

Safeguarding your family means first of all that every mother needs to appreciate how different male and female sexuality are. I only really got it about these differences through frank discussions with my husband and sons following this incident.

What I got is that, because males are so much more affected by visual images, the temptation of pornography can be overwhelming.

It's not like the old days when porn was only available at a seedy little store the next town over. Now it's only as far away as the 7-Eleven or a friend's house, and as near as the computer screen on your desk. While for most women, this isn't a problem, for most men it is.

Getting serious about helping your teen avoid temptation means getting all TVs and computers into the open, out of bedrooms and tucked-away places, and equipping them with filters.

Teach modesty. Understanding male sexuality is vital for parents of teenage girls. Again, because response to visual stimulation is wired into guys, the way girls dress can create difficulties.

Here's how Brandon, a high-school senior from California, put it:

> As a Christian guy, I can say with absolute confidence that the way many girls dress today is a stumbling block for me. I understand that girls want to look their best, and I don't disagree with that, but for me as a guy I can say that looks are not the end all/be all component to a relationship that a girl might be searching for when she wears those types of clothes.

In her excellent book *A Return to Modesty*, Wendy Shalit, a young Jewish college student, describes women as having a natural inclination to modesty. [32] The fact is, in the last two decades, girls have become desensitized to this essential part of their nature.

Again, I draw a contrast between the '80s, when Samantha and her cheerleader friends wore their T-shirts over their bathing suits when guys were around. Many girls today, by contrast, revel in the opportunity to bare their bodies, challenging school dress codes (where there still are such things) with bare midriffs, short skirts, and thong underwear revealed any time they sit down or bend over.

Are guys to blame for getting the wrong idea about girls who dress provocatively? Think about it: When we see a policeman dressed in uniform, we know what he stands for and what to expect. When we see Target employees in khaki pants and red shirts, we know we can ask them where to find the pots and pans.

Girls need to understand that how we present ourselves—not just in dress, but in speech and conduct—paints a picture of who we are. Women need to be careful about the message they are sending.

In discussing date rape, Shalit says:

Today our society makes fun of modesty, and then we are
surprised to find our men behaving abominably. We make fun
of virtue, and then are surprised that men's "amorous expres-
sions" often go "farther than virtue may allow." [33]

Teach your daughters to be responsible in this area by simply saying no.
The other night, in the teen department of our local department store,
I ran into a couple from church. We hadn't been talking long when
their daughter Melanie appeared at the dressing room door to show
them an outfit she was trying on. I was so impressed! Not only Mom
but Dad also was part of her wardrobe decision making. And it was
clear that they had standards they would not be persuaded to abandon.

In our home, all it took was Sophia coming down to the kitchen
one morning in a pair of jeans with cutouts up the side. Her four older
brothers said no loud and clear: "What do you think a guy thinks
when he sees that?" Girls in our family wear one-piece bathing suits
and do not show their midriffs. That's where we've drawn the line.
And once that line was drawn, with an explanation that lets them know
it's based on our love and desire to protect them, it has been easy to
maintain it.

Build a Strong Foundation
Just as we teach our children that sex isn't something evil to say no to,
but something beautiful to wait for—as well as helping them succeed
by preparing them to avoid temptation—we also need to share with
them our vision for the future.

When our children turn thirteen, Tripp takes the birthday boy
camping or I take the birthday girl to a fancy hotel, where we begin
a deep discussion about what it means to be a husband or wife, and

eventually a father or mother. We emphasize that what happens after our marriage vows is unpredictable, using examples they can relate to from real life—such as their oldest brother Joshua's wife Hattie contracting cancer one year into their marriage, which they've been battling together so far for six years; the conflicts that arise following the birth of a child with a disability, as evidenced in the three families whose children we've adopted; the stress of a financial collapse; and the challenge of raising children with special needs, which they've experienced firsthand at home.

Following God's plan for marriage and remaining pure and faithful to one spouse builds a strong foundation that can withstand this kind of pressure, and while some people may fail, God doesn't want us to. He wants to equip us to rise to the challenges that come with being an adult. That's part of his plan.

We ask our children to commit to remaining pure and preserving the special gift God has given them for their future husband or wife. So far, all but one have kept that commitment—and they've all learned from that example, too. While all our children are still close and mutually respectful, there is a sense that this sibling settled for less than all that could have been. Still, God can do wonders with our repentant hearts when we give them to him.

Coming home after this special birthday event doesn't mean the end of the discussion by any means. I'm pleased because my children don't treat sex as a taboo subject, but as something we can talk about and even kid around about—as when my boys somehow think they'll have great sexual prowess because Tripp fathered a lot of kids. Or that a rare night alone means their dad and I will be fooling around, even when I'm recovering from a broken leg.

Having grown up with a background of childhood abuse and later my own promiscuity, and now seeing what it's like for kids raised in a home with an open, healthy attitude about sex, one based on it being a spiritual gift that draws us closer to our spouse and to each other, has been healing for me and has given me great hope for the future generations of our family.

The months leading up to Sophia's wedding to Josh were busy beyond belief. With the wedding only one week after college graduation (well, what do we expect when our kids are faithful to wait until marriage for sex? Of course, they're anxious!), we were not just in the throes of shower dates and wedding plans, but also dealing with a bride- and groom-to-be with senior recitals, projects, exams, and finally graduation.

Sophia came home with her entourage of bridesmaids and friends, and our house became a flurry of femininity: dresses, makeup, high heels, and hairstyles galore, as every social occasion was another excuse to get dressed up. (Liberty University has a strict dress/modesty code, but it is reputed to have the most gorgeous female population around since pretty much everyone there knows they want to get married.) It was great fun, although I felt like the days were slipping through my grasp too quickly. It was one of those many times when, as a parent, you wish you could just make time stop or at least slow down, the better to absorb every single moment.

In-laws arriving, a getting-acquainted dinner, bridal party trip to get the license, bridal shower, bachelor party, rehearsal, rehearsal dinner—every moment was scheduled to keep us busy and moving toward the day every little girl dreams of.

During this time, Sophia sought out the women closest to her—her mom, sisters, sisters-in-law, and friends—to ask us to speak honestly about sex: *What was the first time like? What did she need to know? What did they wish they had known? What advice could they share?* The discussions were frank and full of giggles and anticipation. This helped Sophia immensely, and I was so grateful she had such a healthy attitude and no sense of shame about asking for help.

The night before the wedding, the girls took over our master bedroom, and Tripp and I slept in Maddy's and Sophia's twin beds. Sophia and Maddy shared our big bed, barely sleeping a wink and holding hands all night, saying good-bye to an era in their not-always-easy sisterhood.

In the flurry of the wedding morning we almost forgot the "something borrowed," but we remembered just in time for Sophia's friend Michelle to sew it into the slip of her beautiful miracle/bargain wedding dress: a pocket watch I had given Tripp as a wedding present twenty-nine years before, engraved with "And a time to every purpose under heaven" from Ecclesiastes 3:1. Once again, Tripp and I were reminded that, even though we didn't know God on January 2, 1983, the seeds were there waiting for his timing, and he was already beginning to fulfill his purpose for our lives.

As Tripp came down the aisle with Sophia, I felt moved in many ways: sadness that will always be there that in not understanding the importance of purity I had missed this kind of moment myself; satisfaction for a job well done; and joy that my daughter had made the right choices and was entering her marriage as a pure woman who truly understood what life is all about.

She could have chosen differently, as children of even the most conscientious parents sometimes do. Our children don't always accept what we've taught them. But when we teach them well and they are willing learners, God's best shines through for all to see—as it did that morning in May when the daughter of two casualties of the sexual revolution gave her very best to her husband, their future, and the generations to come.

CHAPTER SEVEN

Submission, Sacrifice, and Service

"Mom, I think I want to try out for *American Idol*."

No matter how many surprises you've had as a mother, there's always room for one more! Here was one from my ninth child, a sophomore in high school. It was a bright early summer afternoon, and Maddy and Jonny had just trudged the half-mile of dirt road between the school bus stop and our country home.

We are a family of singers—not so much Tripp and me, but our kids. When people ask how my kids learned to sing, I tell them the truth: They got their start singing hymns each morning during devotions before homeschool. While I don't play an instrument or have a great voice, I could carry a tune well enough to lead them *a capella*, singing from a bunch of hymnals discarded when our evangelical church got new ones. I preferred the classic hymns to the praise songs that had crowded them out in recent years. The praise songs were all about "me" and "my feelings," while the beautifully written hymns focused more on God's nature and sound theology.

Then there was plenty of singing in church on Sunday, something evangelicals approach with more gusto than Catholics—although I pray one day this will change.

With so many kids, our home was filled with music from morning til night. As Tripp and I realized how much our children loved to sing, we supported their musical talents the same way we supported sports (which for our family included baseball, football, soccer, rugby, and swim team) by investing time, money, and energy in developing their gifts. This meant boys' chorus, church choir, and eventually for a few who wanted more, private voice lessons.

Parents must draw a delicate balance between pushing their own dreams for their kids and simply opening doors that might lead them somewhere God might have plans for them to go. One of the blessings of having so many children has been learning that a child is not someone on whom we put our own stamp—we as parents should never presume that all our children will dance, ride horses, or be math whizzes. I think of my dear son-in-law Kip, who was forced to play piano as a boy and became quite good at it, but the minute he became a man he refused to play at all. On the other hand, our son-in-law Josh recently commented on a Facebook post about a four-year-old piano virtuoso that he wished he had gone farther himself and was sorry to have fought his father about practicing.

See what I mean? It always comes back to that delicate balance.

Once I knew God, I always thought of my children as gifts from him—gifts I had the privilege of watching him unwrap with whatever help he wanted from me. Just as Maria Montessori emphasized "giving the world to the child" in the earliest years, Tripp and I tried hard to introduce not just the things we cherished, but a broader landscape for our children to wander and discover the things they loved. We then observed carefully to see what clicked with each child.

In reality, this meant that if all four boys played Pop Warner Football (because the obvious thing when you have a bunch of boys is to get them in the same place at the same time), and after a year, if one wanted out, that was his choice. Sometimes it's hard not to pressure a child when you hit the wall of your parental aspirations, but this is part of our learning curve as parents: to learn that these children are not ours to mold, but God's. I believe kids will do their best when we drop our own self-interest and listen for the still, small voice of the Holy Spirit.

While our children were as involved in sports as they were in music and theater in the early years, none of them became known for their athletic prowess—although a few of them are big fans of football and baseball (and along the way their formerly uninterested-in-sports dad became a fanatic, too). However, all our kids were known for their voices, and a few have gone on to professional pursuits: musical theater, music ministry, film, and opera. God planted the gifts, we provided opportunities, and because as we were listening for the Holy Spirit we were teaching our children to listen as well, each of our children has found the path God had prepared for their lives.

This doesn't just apply to music, by any means. It applies to my daughters who are wives and mothers, to my son Josh who dropped out of college to build his own contracting company, and to my National Merit Scholar son Zach, who graduated college to become one of those computer geeks who makes a fortune doing something only one other person at the party knows how to talk about.[34] It applies to doctors and nurses who study long and hard to care for us when we are most vulnerable. It applies to the self-sacrificing children of self-sacrificing parents in military families, or to policemen and firemen who put their lives on the line each day to protect and serve. And it applies to our priests, who like Simon of Cyrene carry the cross for us each day—whether or not we are mindful of their sacrifice and their prayers for us.

My point is this: When they place that wriggling, slippery bundle in your arms and together as parents who have participated in a miracle you weep and rejoice and give thanks that he or she is yours, what you will learn along the way is that our children do not really belong to us at all, but to God. This is a truth captured by Kahlil Gibran, a Lebanese-American Eastern Catholic poet, philosopher, and artist, best known for his work *The Prophet*. While some of Gibran's theology may be in dispute, my experience as a mom makes his thoughts on children resonate with me. The whole idea of housing our children's bodies but not their souls is an important concept.

Psalm 127:4–5 says, "Like arrows in the hand of a warrior are the sons of one's youth. Happy is the man who has his quiver full of them!" Consider for a moment the added dimension Gibran brings to this image. The Bible says that our children are our arrows. Gibran adds that we are not the archers, but only the bows—bows in the service of a God who "sees the mark on the path of the infinite" and bends us to aim the arrow (child) where he or she is to go.

Our job? To be flexible in God's hands. To go about our parenting with joy: "Let your bending in the archer's hands be for gladness." And to trust him: "For even as he loves the arrow that flies, so he loves the bow that is stable."

Flexibility, joy, and trust. Perhaps those fruits—which may not have been so obvious in the early years but have grown over forty-some years of parenting—will explain my reaction to Maddy's unexpected whim about *American Idol*.

First, I was curious: We had watched *American Idol* regularly as a family since the very first show, considering it wholesome entertainment (in the early years) with lots of good lessons on how to receive correction and work hard to do your best, but none of my kids had ever been interested in trying out themselves, even when friends urged them to. It just wasn't the kind of music they enjoyed singing; they were more into Broadway musicals. Maddy was interested in jazz, blues, and bluegrass, too—almost anything but pop music.

"Honey, you've always said you wouldn't want to try out for *American Idol*," I said. "What made you change your mind?"

"I don't know. It's just an idea I had on the bus coming home."

One thing Tripp and I have tried to do, especially after adopting children with special needs who've required a little extra from our "normal" kids, is to stretch to meet the needs of our birth children as much as we've learned to stretch to meet the needs of their adopted brothers. In a way, you could say we've learned to be even more flexible and spontaneous than we might have been before.

And so, the very next day my youngest daughter and I were on an eleven-hour ride to Boston, the first of seven audition sites and "coincidentally" the one closest to us. Yes, it was a whim, and yes, it seemed crazy, but I felt irresistibly drawn to go with the flow to see where it might lead. In retrospect, I know that God had a plan, and the nudge Maddy got on the bus that day was the Holy Spirit. Seven months later, when the first episode of *American Idol Season Nine* premiered on TV, our family could see that when God is in charge and we are obedient, he can use even the most worldly vehicle for his purposes.

Having received wristbands and instructions the day before, seven thousand Boston hopefuls—each one with a parent or friend in tow—obediently began lining up at Fenway Park on a cold and rainy Friday morning at 4:00 A.M. Spirits were high and songs were in the air; these were kids who love to entertain, after all. But by the time the gates to the stadium finally opened at 10:00 A.M., everyone was drenched, and the would-be Beyonces and Rihannas in full diva regalia were beside themselves trying to restore at least a vestige of their glamour.

Easygoing Maddy—as usual, *au naturel* in Birkenstocks, beaded bracelets, and long curly hair—didn't have as much to worry about.

Seated at one side of the stadium, we began a day of waiting. Ryan Seacrest came in and led us in cheers and chants—our first peek into what goes into the making of a TV show, as we were instructed to smile more, yell more, wave more, and keep generating that enthusiasm for take after take.

People love to hear the inside scoop: Do they actually listen to every singer there? Yes, but what you see on TV is a condensation of months of behind-the-scenes, involving several trips to the audition city and many levels of producers before the TV judges. That first day there were a dozen gazebos across the field from us, and at each gazebo sat a few producers who listened for thirty seconds to each singer before judging whether to bestow a Golden Ticket—at this stage not the Golden Ticket to Hollywood, but a ticket to return to Boston a month later for the next round.

Out of seven thousand hopefuls, Maddy was one of a hundred who made it through, and that hundred included the ones *American Idol* would be playing for laughs. When we returned to Boston a month later, we were encouraged to bring other family members, so Maddy and I brought two of her brothers with Down syndrome, her "Irish twin" brother, Jonny, and our youngest adopted son, Justin. For three days, Maddy sang for higher and higher levels of judges and filmed interviews while other singers were eliminated. The final day, she was ushered into the familiar TV judges where she sang a couple verses of Leonard Cohen's "Hallelujah." All four judges were unanimous in awarding her the real Golden Ticket to Hollywood.

When she came through the door dejectedly, she didn't fool me for an instant. We were all hugging and jumping up and down just as we'd seen others do so many times before. The look on Ryan Seacrest's face when Jonny threw his arms around him was priceless.

This was in August, and we wouldn't be going to Hollywood until January. In September we were surprised when the producers called for permission to come and visit and film our family for a day. We agreed and spent a delightful day with a production crew and cameras. Then, since contestants could lose their contract for breaking secrecy agreements, we went about our lives as usual. Finally, in January, we were flown to Hollywood to begin competition with contestants from all over the country. Because Maddy was under eighteen, she had to have a parent in tow at all times, more music to my adventure-loving heart.

There were about two hundred contestants in Hollywood, and I verified a theory I'd had about *American Idol* that the most of the contestants were believers. As we waited in the holding rooms for whatever was next on the schedule, here and there someone would pull out a guitar and break into a worship song, gathering a large group of devoted singers. Black contestants sang gospel. Performers prayed in groups large and small. All were supportive of each other.

Maddy was up for the first round of Hollywood judging on the same night that *American Idol* was airing its first show of the season, which the producers told us would include special footage of her family. Since she was on the Kodak Theater stage and I was in the audience, we didn't see the show as it aired. But ironically, just as America was seeing Maddy featured as the first contestant to win the Golden Ticket to Hollywood, she was actually being eliminated when the judges didn't like her song choice: Ella Fitzgerald's "The Nearness of You."

It had been a long journey, and Maddy cried when goaded by the cameramen: "So, how do you feel?" We fled upstairs to our room to discover Maddy's name in the top ten Google searches and to see for ourselves what viewers around the country had seen that night:[35] A video of the crowd at the initial auditions, followed by Maddy and her brothers coloring together as she waited for her August audition, and then Maddy being interviewed about her family, especially her close bond with her Down syndrome brothers. "I think some people are a little skeptical of people with Down syndrome. Those four boys bring out the best in every person they meet. They see the world in colors— and we need to see the world in colors too," she is quoted as saying. The video of her actual audition followed, including the judges' reactions, and excited hugs in the waiting room by Ryan, Jonny, Justin, and me.

Both Maddy and I were filled with a profound sense of peace. As she was brushing her teeth, there was a knock at the door and I peeped out to see a camera crew—a frequent occurrence, as hours of footage are shot of every contestant.

"Please don't answer the door, Mom." I understood. Our mission was accomplished.

But the crew showing up only underscored the miracle that had just taken place. Since her audition, Maddy had been on camera constantly. And out of all that film footage, *American Idol* had chosen to present a beautiful portrait of a wholesome and unselfish young girl from a big family who loved her brothers with Down syndrome. Honestly, when you're a parent who's been advocating for kids with special needs for many years, it doesn't get much better than that.

Left on the cutting room floor was Maddy's remark that 90 percent of babies diagnosed prenatally with Down syndrome are aborted (even though she remembers it made the producer cry), but intact was a strong pro-life message—not in the form of a sermon, but in the story of one person's life. I would never have dreamed of praying that God would give such a boost to families affected by Down syndrome on national TV. But I didn't have to. He had a plan to do it, and all it required was the cooperation of a sixteen-year-old girl on a school bus.

As a result of this national exposure, Maddy was able to stage a one-woman show to raise relief money for the Haiti earthquake that occurred while we were in Hollywood. She also went on to a year of speaking and singing at pro-life events, culminating in the 2011 March for Life Rally at the Verizon Center before an audience of 22,000 pro-life teens.

Today she is at Catholic University studying opera (following in the footsteps of opera singer Ben, in grad school at Eastman University). And though she had a chance to return to *American Idol* two years later, she turned it down, saying it would be a distraction.

This is a long story with a major point: I cannot emphasize enough the importance of listening for the still, small voice of the Holy Spirit as you grow in your parenting journey. Only then can you teach your children to listen as well. What we refer to as the "still, small voice" may not sound like a voice, at least not most of the time. It's usually more of a gentle nudge in a certain direction. It can be very subtle, and the first few times you obey it, you will be taking a leap of faith. You may not know right away if you did the right thing or not. It can take weeks, months—sometimes years—to know for sure. But when it is revealed, you will see God's hand in directing you and creating something beautiful out of your obedience.

If our children are going to be ready to listen for and obey the still, small voice of God, they will get there by learning to listen to and obey their parents. In today's culture, the word obedience is not as respected as it once was. This goes hand in hand with the confusion of parents being pals, discussed in chapter three. When our children grow up we can become friends, but when they are young we have to be parents. Children need to know that there is someone in charge—a loving authority. Mothers and fathers are representatives of God, and unfortunately, adults who grow up in dysfunctional homes often have dysfunctional ideas about who God is. As mothers and fathers, we all fall short, but for our children's sake, we must strive to be worthy representatives of the Father of us all.

Children being obedient used to be so understood throughout society that even little children learned games like Mother, May I? and Red Light, Green Light—games which gave children practice in obeying a command. All in the context of fun, of course, but that kind of self-control is an early building block that grows with the child and can be transferred to other aspects of life.

In my opinion, it also helps to require children to say "Yes, Sir" and "No, Ma'am"—a practice still common in the South, but fading in other parts of the country.

We are created to love and serve God, and the way we do that is to love and serve our fellow man. The place the child learns that first is in the Domestic Church, at home with his or her family. So while parents are not pals, the family is still a team of interdependent individuals who share a common purpose: to love and serve each other—and when that love is multiplied, to take it into the world.

Gary Chapman's helpful bestseller, *The 5 Love Languages*, presents the idea that each of us has the tendency to show our own love and respond to the others in a particular way: through words of affirmation, gifts, quality time, acts of service, and physical touch.[36] (Note to parents: Like the introversion/extroversion types discussed in chapter three, this is another important tool for understanding what makes your child tick and identifying possible sources of conflict within the family. All of these are worthy of ongoing family discussions, to help everyone appreciate their differences and strive for harmony within the family.)

My own personal love language involves acts of service—both giving and receiving. Beyond that, I believe that service is the mandate Jesus left for us. Before the Last Supper, he girded himself with a towel and knelt before each of the disciples to wash their filthy feet (and in those days with sandals and dusty roads, we can be pretty sure they *were* filthy), setting an example for us to follow. True service calls for us to go beyond the mechanical carrying out of a job to a deep, personal involvement of love for those we serve.

A family generates a lot of work, and in this day and age, with smaller families and professional household help, the tendency may be for children to do less, yet it is vital for their emotional health and spiritual growth that they learn to work with love.

Seven Strategies to Build a Strong Work Ethic in Your Children

From an early age, children need to work in order to meet their God-given potential. A child gains confidence and spiritual graces from being of service. The ability to work hard, to tolerate frustration, and to take responsibility doesn't just happen without a commitment from his or her parents. To get your children off to the best start, here are seven guidelines:

1. Start Early

Don't count on school to mold your child into a good worker. The groundwork is laid well before kindergarten. While developing her educational method, Dr. Maria Montessori observed the intense desire of toddlers to be productive, to imitate adult work. She noted "sensitive periods" when a child is most open to certain skills. She believed that when teachers

and parents understand these periods and respond appropriately, learning is filled with joy.

Think of your three-year-old begging to peel carrots, or your
four-year-old pleading to mop the floor. While our tendency
is to tell them they're not ready, Montessori would say their
desire is our invitation to teach them now.

The secret to allowing your child to help with a difficult task
is to break it down into small steps, and this requires patience.
Children who have the opportunity to serve when they ask
will be more likely to step up to a task later on.

2. Accept What You Get

Naturally, letting a four-year-old mop the floor means your
floor won't get very clean. Still, it's important to graciously
praise the effort and the desire to help, not the results.

For example, seven-year-old Bella decided to surprise her
mom by cleaning the dining room windows. After all, she'd
seen her brother washing them, and it looked pretty easy.
When Bella's mom saw the far-from-perfect results, she
ignored the smudges and smears.

"What a lovely job!" she said simply, "I love to clean
windows, too. Next time let's do it together!"

As a result, Bella felt like a real helper and couldn't wait to
do more household chores.

3. Know Your Children

Children are individuals and mature at different rates. As your
child takes on new chores and responsibilities, strike a balance

between accepting his best effort and raising the bar to challenge him as his capacity grows. Pay attention to where your child is developmentally. There's a difference between a five-year-old who hasn't noticed that plates have two sides and a ten-year-old who neglects to wash the backs because he's in a hurry to get outside and play. One needs teaching; the other needs accountability.

Parents also need to know how to motivate each child. Young children are often motivated by verbal praise. Emphasize how much your child's work helps you and others.

Older children need more. During this stage, money and increased freedom become the main motivators. There's nothing wrong with children getting paid for their efforts—after all, we get paid for ours—but ideally we all need to learn to do our best just because it's the right thing to do. Even if you pay your kids for some chores, there should be a few household tasks they do simply because they're part of the family. If you don't want to offer money for chores, use added privilege as an incentive.

4. Teach Delayed Gratification

Let's face it, living in a me-first culture requires an extra effort from parents to help children develop thoughtfulness and self-control—two traits that will be essential for avoiding the temptations of the teen years.

It starts by establishing a pattern: We work, and then we play. You might say to your child, "I know you want to play. Let's pick up all these blocks and fold the clothes, and then we can go outside together." Or, "Let's get the house cleaned up, and then we'll make some popcorn and watch a movie."

We've found that teaching delayed gratification means creating obstacles when things come a little too easily. Shortly before Josh's sixteenth birthday, his grandma told us she planned to buy herself a new car and give him her Jeep. We asked her instead to charge him $500—not the full value of the car but a hefty chunk from his savings. As a result he took better care of the Jeep than he might have had it been a freebie.

5. Equip Them to Earn

Through the years we've given our kids a base allowance, then awarded bonuses for work done well and cheerfully. We've also encouraged them to find other ways to earn money.

One year four of our boys—then ages seven to twelve—raised rats to sell to pet stores. We taught them to keep records and understand the language of business: expenses, income, profits, and losses.

Later, they all had once-a-week paper routes. The boys learned a lot about customer service, human nature, persistence, and patience.

As teenagers, they started a company called Brothers Firewood and spent the winter splitting and delivering firewood.

What all of these ventures had in common was that they took an enormous amount of time and energy—mine and their dad's! Nurturing their entrepreneurial spirit meant schlepping the boys and a fresh batch of rats to the pet store every few weeks, or driving them on their paper routes when it was soggy outside, or rehearsing how to handle nonpaying customers. For my husband, it meant driving a truck loaded with wood until Josh got his license and teaching the kids how to take responsibility for a dented mailbox even when it meant losing money on a delivery.

Help your kids find work they'll enjoy, and you won't have to push them out the door to do it. You'll undoubtedly have to offer a little work of your own to get them started. If your child wants to rake leaves, be ready to knock on doors with him. If she wants to walk dogs, help her place an ad in the paper. Be ready and willing to help your child start working, and you'll be amazed at the life lessons she'll learn.

6. Encourage Volunteering

Teaching a child to enjoy earning money is a good thing, but teaching him to enjoy service for its own sake is best.

Today volunteerism is trendy. More and more schools—both private and public—are requiring hours of volunteer work from students each semester. For Christians, volunteerism holds a special resonance, as it means following the Jesus's command to love and serve.

When your children are young, find ways to involve them in your own service projects. Let them help when you deliver a meal to a new mom or bring flowers to an elderly friend. Talk about how Christ laid down his life for us and discuss the small ways in which we do that for others. You can pick up trash on your street or on the beach, visit convalescent homes, or pull weeds for a next-door neighbor.

As your children get older, help them find other ways to serve. They can go on a short-term mission trips, help serve lunch at a soup kitchen, or volunteer with the Special Olympics. This is truly being salt and light, and it should be part of any Christian's work ethic.

7. Be a Role Model

So much of who our children turn out to be is a reflection not of what we try to pour into them but of what they see in us. It's not the big occasions our kids will remember most, but the everyday stuff that revealed what their parents were really made of: how we handled frustration, whether we were generally on time, whether we kept commitments, and whether we did our own work with a smile or a frown.

Like all good things, building a strong work ethic in your child takes constant effort. But you'll know it's worth it when your child comes home from the first day of his first job looking tired and satisfied and grown-up, saying something like my oldest son Josh said to me after his first day working for a "real" company: "My boss said I did a good job, Mom. Thanks for everything."

For some parents, the first obstacle in teaching their children a love of submission and service may be that they haven't made peace with it themselves. And isn't that the glorious thing about parenting? Without taking vows which would have meant that we forego a family, we still have plenty of opportunities to practice spiritual discipline—all the better to serve those whom God has placed in our care.

Let me give you a few sources of my own inspiration—from the ridiculous to the sublime. Don't forget that, as a mom, I was often teaching myself the basic lessons as I taught them to my children.

Consider the dwarves in Disney's *Snow White:* They spend their days in the mines, singing about how they like to "dig, dig, dig." The dwarves loved digging, but they hated housework. Snow White transforms their domestic disaster with the cheerful help of forest friends who teach them to whistle while they work, thus demonstrating the power of love to make cleaning house a transcendent experience.

We can learn to love work too, heeding the advice of artist Mary Engelbreit, whose happy housewife tango—rose in mouth, vacuum in one hand, and feather duster in the other—appears under the banner, "To be happy, don't do what you like, like what you do."

Our culture's work hierarchy sells us short by sneering at work like flipping burgers (which, after all, has built good job habits into a million workers), as though we should judge people by *what* they do rather than *how* they do it. I've met burger-flippers who would put many CEOs to shame.

I don't think God ranks our work at all. I don't think he values neurosurgeons more than janitors, or airplane pilots more than parking-lot attendants, or U.S. senators over stay-at-home moms. In fact, judging by what he has told us, those who do the most lowly and unappreciated work find greater favor in God's sight. After all, God has great love for "the least of these." And no fewer than seven passages, in three of the four Gospels, remind us that the first shall be last, as in Matthew 20:26–28:

Whoever would be great among you must be your servant, and whoever would be first among you must be your slave; even as the Son of man came not to be served but to serve, and to give his life as a ransom for many.

Does this mean that someone in a high position or with a status-packed job can't find favor with God? Not at all. It all depends on attitude.

I think of the pediatric surgeon twenty years ago who treated a tiny baby with Down syndrome as if he were a crown prince and his worried parents as if they were all that mattered in his busy day. Only later did we learn that Michael Harrison was famous for his work in pioneering prenatal surgery. To me, he is a living example of the way God intends us to pursue our calling—with humility and grace.

Unfortunately, we don't see the combination of high status and humility as often as we should. This explains why Jesus told his disciples, "It is easier for a camel to go through the eye of a needle than for a rich man to enter the kingdom of God" (Matthew 19:24). He didn't say it was impossible, just that it was exceedingly difficult.

My own daily work runs the gamut from cleaning up kids' messes to the privilege of writing a book like this in hopes of passing on some of what I've learned to others. I keep before me the idea that both are equally important in God's eyes—and that cleaning messes may actually be more important because only God sees it.

Yes, work is indeed a love language. But it's a love language only if the one working—or serving—has the right attitude about what they do.

As Kahlil Gibran, again from *The Prophet*, says: "Work is love made visible."[37] He went on to say that if you bake a loaf of bread with indifference, it becomes a "bitter bread" that only feeds "half a man's hunger."

Being a Christian has taken me beyond the prejudices of the world to a more godly perspective of work. Becoming Catholic, with Our Blessed Mother and all the saints as role models of submission, has refined those lessons and helped me to understand that the fulfillment of our specific calling is our gift to God.

I want to work because I love—and I love even more because I worked. And I want to pass on everything I've learned so that my children (and yours, if this resonates with you) will grow gracefully in submission, sacrifice, and service as it flows from deep within their hearts, where God planted the seeds their parents have nurtured.

· · ·

CHAPTER EIGHT

For Such a Time as This

Once upon a time there was a young maiden who lived, like all the members of her religion, scattered among those who did not share her faith. Encouraged by her guardian uncle, she entered a beauty contest to find a new queen for a king angry at his first wife's disobedience. As in every good fairy tale, the beautiful young woman—who otherwise might have lived her life unnoticed—won the palace and the crown.

But the "happily ever after" didn't happen the way it should. When, because of his beliefs, the new queen's uncle refused to bow to the king's official, the official ordered that the uncle and all who shared his religion be killed. In desperation, the uncle asked his royal niece to intercede, but she worried for her life—and perhaps for revealing her religious identity. The king saw no one save through his own summons, and he hadn't summoned her for a month.

The uncle replied that the lives of their people hung in the balance. And though his faith made him secure that, despite many lost lives, the deliverance of their entire tribe would somehow come from another place, he chided the young queen: "Who knows whether you have not come to the kingdom for such a time as this?"

I love that question. And I love the book it comes from. For the story I referred to is not a fairy tale at all, but the book of Esther in the Bible. This story—which never mentions God by name though his presence hovers over the story in a very special way—is her story. And what is remarkable about Esther is her submission and obedience to a call which might have seemed more worldly than of God—it was a beauty contest, after all—but which God had somehow established as a way to secure the living stream of his chosen people, the Jews.

One of the things I love about Catholicism is the way our faith is a continuation of that of the Jews. Jesus is our Messiah, but our roots go back farther than that, as we are reminded at the Easter Vigil each year. The Church did not spring into being when one or another reformer came along and finally got it right. It came through Jesus Christ and included the legacy of God's chosen people who came before, although Our Savior's redemption would open the gates to Jews and Gentiles alike.

I'm not a theologian—I prefer to keep my faith simple and child-like—but I think this is an important distinction of the Catholic faith. Though some Catholic subgroups (similar to some rigid Protestant groups) may add extra-biblical rules and structures that might discourage a godly young woman called to enter a beauty contest, there is really nothing in our faith that would discourage following the Holy Spirit wherever we are led.

We are a Church that flows from a fisherman, the very man chosen by God as our first pope. Our Bible is filled with stories of sinners whose obedience to God redeemed their lives and the lives of others.

God Can Use You—No Excuses!

The next time you think God can't use you, just look to the Bible to see what he had to work with:

- Noah was a drunk (Genesis 9:21)

- Abraham was too old (Genesis 17:17)
- Jacob was a liar (Genesis 27)
- Leah was ugly (Genesis 29:16–18)
- Joseph was abused (Genesis 37:22–28)
- Moses had a stuttering problem (Exodus 4:10)
- Gideon was afraid (Judges 6:15) (I'm not entirely sure about this reference.)
- Samson had long hair and was a womanizer (Judges 16:5, 17)
- Rahab was a harlot (Joshua 2:1)
- Jeremiah and Timothy were too young (Jeremiah 1:6)
- David had an affair and was a murderer (2 Samuel 11:2–4; 14–17)
- Elijah was suicidal (1 Kings 19:4)
- Isaiah preached naked (Isaiah 20:2)
- Jonah ran from God (Jonah 1:3)
- Naomi was a widow (Ruth 1:3)
- Job went bankrupt (Job 1:21)
- Peter denied Christ (Mark 14:71)
- The disciples fell asleep while praying (Mathew 26:40)
- Martha worried about everything (Luke 10:40–42)
- The Samaritan woman was divorced, more than once (John 4:17–18)
- Zacchaeus was too small (Luke 19:2–3)
- Paul was too religious (Galatians 1:14)
- Timothy had an ulcer (1Timothy 5:23)
- Lazarus was dead (John 11)

What does this have to do with being parents? Everything—because most of us come into parenthood with a less-than-sterling past. Some of us enter parenthood carrying a lot of baggage, still recovering from damaged childhoods or wasted young adulthoods. Some are without a clue about God or much thought about the future. Some have rejected a Church they did not understand.

Some enter parenthood like Tripp and I; they find themselves pregnant. Though we did not know God when this happened, he knew us. The thought of abortion never crossed our minds, and we married six days after receiving the news that I was pregnant. Tripp jokes, "God pulled a shotgun wedding," but the joke holds a kernel of truth. Although it would be five years before we knew God, He led two sinners past another sin and gave us our first son, Joshua Gabriel. Each year on Josh's birthday, we acknowledge that his birth was the cornerstone on which our family is built. Is it something to be ashamed of? Not anymore, since God redeemed our lives once we submitted them to him.

It hasn't all been a bed of roses, by any means, but it has been worth it. I can't imagine any other calling so greatly challenging and refining us as believers. Parenthood has proven to be the perfect spiritual training ground, calling us each day to die to ourselves and our own desires. Motherhood has required a surrender and dependence on God that has allowed him to reveal me as he always intended me to be. This process, which has been going on for the forty-three years I have been a parent, even before I became a Christian, reminds me of the story of Michelangelo. When asked how he created his masterpiece statue of the young man with a slingshot on the verge of slaying a giant, he said simply, "I chipped away everything that wasn't David."

God saw what no one else could see inside the hard stone of my heart. In his loving and skillful hands, all that was not me has been (and is still being) steadily chipped away. At times I thought I had met the limits of my endurance—as when our eighth child Jonny was born not only with Down syndrome but with medical problems which kept us in and out of the hospital for fifteen months, or when our second son left home at eighteen—as the Creator of All, he knew—and has always been able to perfectly gauge—just how much stress I can handle without crumbling completely.

> I thought parenting was going to portray my strength, never realizing that God had ordained it to reveal my weaknesses.[38]
>
> —Dave Harvey

But there have also been the joyful, transcendent moments when the gift of raising children—and the special gift of raising lots of them—lifted me into a higher realm than I'd ever imagined. Like Eric Liddell, the devout Olympic runner immortalized in the movie *Chariots of Fire*, who said, "When I run, I feel God's pleasure," I too know the joy of discovering my calling and fulfilling it in obedience to a God who understands me better than I understand myself.

Do I sound like a cheerleader? Well, yes, I guess I do, and yes, I guess I am. Once I settled down, married Tripp, acknowledged the sin and shortcomings of my early motherhood, and began trying to make the world a better place through raising emotionally and spiritually healthy children, my focus shifted to unburdening, enlightening, equipping, and empowering other parents to raise a stronger generation to come. This is really the only thing that gives me the courage to write. After all, there are a lot of parenting books out there. Does the world really need another?

The problem is that the experts who write many of those parenting books add burdens to an already challenging task. But Jesus made it clear that this is not what the Christian life is all about when he said:

Come to me, all who labor and are heavy laden, and I will give you rest; Take my yoke upon you and learn from me, for I am gentle and lowly in heart; and you will find rest for your souls. For my yoke is easy, and my burden is light. (Matthew 11:28–30)

If I thought for a moment that the words in this book would add one ounce more to any parent's burden, I would stop writing and take up gardening—even though all my plants somehow seem to end up huddled in a corner of the porch on suicide watch. I'm not good at raising flowers, but because I wanted so much to please God in the area of parenting and because I had so many children, I think I've learned a lot about raising children.

My advice to all parents is to follow the lead of the Holy Spirit in choosing what to parenting books to read, avoiding rigid and legalistic systems which will only burden you and complicate your relationship with your children and the simple, trusting relationship God wants to have with them. When you do choose something to read, see if it resonates with your own wisdom and experience, and feel free to toss out anything that does not ring true to the character of God as a just and loving Father.

I am not one for flying-by-the-seat-of-your-pants parenting. I think it's important for every parent to have a plan and a vision. Spending time reading, praying, and discussing parenting is far more important than studying 401K plans (Have you ever noticed how Sunday morning radio is filled with these financial talk shows—a clear picture of the "Choose this day who you will serve" paradigm?)

Yes, we should all have ideals. But ideals aren't something to use to beat yourself up about, measuring how you are falling short; rather they should be a source of inspiration. You are in charge, accountable only to God. I believe he wants us to let our ideals lift us up, not weigh us down.

On the other hand, there is honest conviction—for instance, when we discover some new perspective on parenting and realize that it is something we should be doing, or perhaps should have been doing for a long time, we may receive a nudge from the Holy Spirit and honestly acknowledge that we've fallen short and need to change.

How can we tell if what we hear or feel is the still, small voice of the Holy Spirit or the whisper of the Great Discourager? I've been through both scenarios myself, and I believe I've discovered a simple test to find the answer: The Great Discourager will use our shortcomings and failures to hit below the belt, leaving us weak and demoralized. He knows that guilt cripples. On the other hand, God knows that, too, so when the Holy Spirit brings conviction, we may grieve, but we also look forward to forging ahead and getting it right. This is something we might not see right away but will find when we take our regrets to the Lord.

Remember: God wants us to succeed—after all, his children are in our hands.

> For I know the plans I have for you, says the Lord, plans for welfare and not for evil, to give you a future and a hope.
> —Jeremiah 29:11

His children are in our hands, and our hope and future will be in theirs. We're raising not only the next generation of children but the next generation of parents—who, in turn, will be inspired by the way they were raised to do their best, too. In this way, even our simplest choices take on greater significance, as what we do and say today will resonate through generations to come.

We live in perilous times—we are facing the persecution of Catholics around the globe, including threats to our religious freedom here in the United States. We live in corrupt times, with our children growing up, as Peggy Noonan wrote,[39] swimming like little fish in polluted waters, poisoned by casual violence, materialism, secularism, anti-life sentiment, and the "pornification of culture—a term coined by Baptist-to-Catholic convert Laura Ingraham that kind of says it all.

We can't remove them completely from that stream, though many of us are guided by the Holy Spirit to do our best to provide a sheltered homeschooling environment and eliminate or seriously limit entertainment choices. It's much like raising plants in a hothouse until they are strong enough to endure the larger world. Yet the world still creeps in through grocery checkout lines, billboards, and friends in the neighborhood. Good parents can only pray a hedge of God's protection around their children to keep their hearts and minds sound.

Eventually, however, parental control comes to an end and children will face the real world. The way the Holy Spirit led our family was to build that bridge gradually rather than risk a sudden shift from the safe haven of the home to the insecurity and hyper-stimulation of the greater world, a world without boundaries. We wanted to walk alongside our children as they found their own boundaries. We didn't want them to decide someday that their faith was that of their parents and never really their own.

Tripp and I believed in the might and mercy of God—after all, we were living proof that God could draw us out of darkness and into light. Although we spent the first twelve years of our Christian walk homeschooling and building a strong faith foundation in our children, we responded as the Holy Spirit nudged us towards more involvement in the world. This took some faith, but it was a faith that went beyond our own work as parents to embrace the words of our Lord:

> You are the salt of the earth; but if salt has lost its taste, how shall its saltiness be restored? It is no longer good for anything except to be thrown out and trodden under foot by men. You are the light of the world. A city set on a hill cannot be hid. Nor do men light a lamp and put it under a bushel, but on a stand, and it gives light to all in the house. Let your light so shine before men, that they may see your good works and give glory to your Father who is in heaven. (Matthew 5:13–16)

What I didn't realize then but have since realized through my own experience and by observing other families is that sheltering your children too much or for too long can be as damaging as not providing enough shelter or letting them go too soon. While I don't believe in following the world in terms of early dating, I also think that parents who keep an overly tight control over their children until they leave home have not adequately prepared their children to withstand worldly temptations or have not shown them what it means to be salt and light.

Think about it: When your child is learning to walk, you have to let go, and she has to fall. It's part of the process. When you teach your child to drive, you don't just suddenly give him the wheel; instead, you sit beside him as he learns to become an aware and wise driver. He starts out driving in empty parking lots, followed by small safe trips, with you gauging when he will be ready to drive over a bridge, onto a freeway, or into the city. Through it all, he makes mistakes, and you discuss them. Every learning process is like this—we don't learn from success; we learn through our mistakes.

Many well-intentioned parents don't allow their teens the freedom to make a mistake, to hear from the Holy Spirit themselves. I'm not talking about the big issues here—like sex before marriage or drugs and alcohol. I'm referring to things that may damage their innocence a little and leave a few scars—leaving them stronger in the knowledge that what their parents taught them was right after all.

Let's take this from theory to my own experience:

Maddy was seventeen. She'd been brought up on a wide range of movies—as discussed in chapter four—everything from silent films, black and white classics, foreign films, and documentaries, all run through the filter of Tripp's and my movie sensibilities.

I love movies for their ability to teach values through stories—not in a preaching way, but with humor and fun. *Groundhog Day*, for instance, has so much to say about the daily choices we have regarding selfish behavior and specific acts of love and compassion. I believe that, when it comes to entertainment, if you introduce a wholesome diet of music and movies early in children's lives, in any confrontation, the good within them will prove more attractive than any outer evil.

"But all my friends are going to see it," Maddy began as usual, this time about *Black Swan*, a recent favorite with serious film critics and the artsy crowd. Indeed, it was just the kind of film that once upon a time would have been top priority for me.

"Have you read the reviews, Maddy? This doesn't sound like something you would want to see. Lots of darkness and despair," I said, fully expecting that this would matter to her. After all, Maddy has always been the most upbeat and positive person I know, pure of heart and spirit. Her favorite films are pre-1960 black-and-white movies, and her favorite singer is Doris Day. She often says she feels like she was born in the wrong era. There is not a drop of angst in her.

"But, Mom, it's very artistic, and I think I can handle it."

"It's R-rated, Maddy," I tried again, but of course Maddy reminded me that I'd taught her to judge films based on their merit rather than the MPAA ratings.

"And besides, I'm seventeen, so I can see R-rated movies," she said. "I have to start making my own decisions at some point. What about when I go to college?"

Here is where many well-intentioned parents might fall back on something like, "Well, as long as you're under our roof, you have to go by our rules." And while that may be perfect for some situations, I just didn't feel it was right in this case. For one thing, my daughter had been honest with me, and I'd rather keep that important part of our relationship. For another, I think it's important to distinguish between the Really-Big-No issues like sex and drugs, and those that don't have such grave consequences.

"Maddy, I know you better than anyone in the world. I know you've never liked darkness and scary themes, that sometimes the images of even the most subtle old murder mysteries have disturbed you more than they might others. I've seen a lot of supposedly artistic movies like *Black Swan*, but I can tell you that this is not going to be your cup of tea. I'm telling you because I love you, and I want to help you avoid something you may regret."

But the still, small voice had already given me peace about the decision I knew she was headed for. I knew that what I said was true, but that this was going to be a situation where my daughter would learn from experience; it was not the mountain on which I wanted our unusually close relationship to die.

And so off she went.

I was sick that day—coughing and wheezing through the whole conversation, Vicks still smeared on my chest from the night before, ready to crawl back into bed as soon as I could take a break from being mom. Instead, I bundled up and headed for the cinemaplex—different theater, same movie. I huddled there in the dark crunching cough drops and experiencing *Black Swan* through three perspectives: my former artsy self, my new-creature-in-Christ eyes, and those of my daughter.

My purpose was to be prepared to talk about the movie when Maddy came home—not just from reading the reviews on the Christian watchdog sites but actually seeing it for myself. I wanted our conversation to be as real and authentic as it could be, not just something to be chalked up to an overly protective parent. The movie exceeded my expectations—full of darkness, depravity, and despair.

Maddy came home from the movie and went straight to her room, her silence speaking volumes. At dinner, her dad asked her about the movie and got a noncommittal answer. I wanted Maddy to bring it up herself, but when she didn't, I waited until after her younger brothers were in bed. That's when I told her that I had gone to see the movie too.

"Why, Mom?" she asked.

"Because I love you, and I wanted to be able to talk about it from an informed perspective. I couldn't just go by what other people said; I had to see it for myself."

"It was the most depressing thing I ever saw," Maddy said. "I'm glad I saw it only because I would never make a mistake like that again."

This was the Holy Spirit at work—a Holy Spirit we can trust to work inside the hearts of our children just as he works in our own. I felt affirmed for this reason: Maddy had the opportunity to step outside the boundaries of the values her parents had always enforced, and now, because of her experience, she made them her own. Had she had this first test after she left home for college, coming back to a dorm full of distractions and worldly perspectives, she might have just accepted this as part of her new freedom—the new normal for her as an adult. And it might have made it easier to give into other temptations, like having sex "because everyone else is."

Now, three years later, our relationship is still close, and trusting enough that I am confident when I say she has never seen another movie like *Black Swan*. With a century of wonderful movies out there (we recently caught a big-screen fifty-year anniversary special of *Singing in the Rain* and were blown away by a true movie classic that will live forever), why settle for anything less than the best?

Does my daughter sound like a nerd because she's close to her family and embraces the values we taught her? By no means! Maddy's a gorgeous blonde, loaded with charisma and lots of friends. She sometimes wears her skirts a little short, her jeans a little tight, but again, at nineteen she needs to make her own choices, and we won't bug her unless they are the big, important ones. Which is why she respects our opinion when we try to put the kibosh on a prospective boyfriend who we can see falls way short.

Maddy respects her parents and trusts our opinion. She loves to have fun, but not to party or go clubbing. These things set her apart—and her peers may not understand—but they don't detract from her likeability.

This is what we hope for when we teach our children that yes, indeed we are different, we are set apart. Because of our faith, our lives should look different—not because of the way we dress, but because our lives reflect the joy found only when our hearts are pure and our lives are dedicated to serving God in whatever calling he has for us.

Maddy is our ninth child, so I have to admit that she is the beneficiary of many more years of experience than some of our earlier children were. And if it seems that I have focused more on Sophia and Maddy in the pages of this book, it's because our other children were already grown when I started writing this one, and their stories have been told in my other books.

Relaying stories about my own parenting is not meant to boost my own stature as a mother, for I hope you can sense that I have my share of regrets and I-wish-I'd-known-sooners. But with many children, I have many stories—and I tell stories to encourage you to find and tell *your* stories. As Jesus taught through parables, we can learn from looking at our own experiences with our children to see what stories we have to tell. It's through this understanding—finding the bigger picture, the moral, the meaning, whatever God has to teach us—that we can learn to be better parents and pass this quality of self-awareness and self-improvement on to our children.

As Catholic parents, unless we make a conscious decision to withdraw our family from the world (which God may certainly call some families to do), we will spend many years rubbing elbows with a wide variety of people with a wide assortment of beliefs and values. The challenge then is this: We have a responsibility to be *in* the world but not *of* it—channels through which the light and life and love of God shine—and give our children the confidence in their faith to do the same.

Purposeful parenting takes a lot of work, but it also takes a lot more grace than many parenting experts understand. It's the grace that comes from making mistakes and learning to trust God to make up the difference between our own best efforts and his incomparable love.

How could I ever repay God for picking up a lost little girl and making something worthy of my life, for seeing who I could be and how I might be able to serve others? The truth is I can't, except through these words, written in love to other mothers like me. And except through prayers that God might use these words to plant and water the seeds he planted and watered in me in the next generation of mothers—mothers who will then find the joy of raising God-first kids in a me-first world.

Is the burden of parenting harder for us now than it was for parents of the past? As someone who has raised two generations of children, my observation is that it certainly seems that way. But what I can say for certain is that God has a plan—and if we trust him, he will guide us through these difficult times. The future depends on how truly we can commit to raise the next generation. We're here for such a time as this.

1. The 12 Steps of Alcoholics Anonymous are such helpful tools for living—surrender, self-honesty, forgiveness, making amends, spiritual growth—that I love to share them more widely. *The Big Book of* Alcoholics Anonymous provides specific directions for each of these:

   1. We admitted we were powerless over alcohol—that our lives had become unmanageable.
   2. Came to believe that a Power greater than ourselves could restore us to sanity.
   3. Made a decision to turn our will and our lives over to the care of God as we understood Him.
   4. Made a searching and fearless moral inventory of ourselves.
   5. Admitted to God, to ourselves, and to another human being the exact nature of our wrongs.
   6. Were entirely ready to have God remove all these defects of character.
   7. Humbly asked Him to remove our shortcomings.
   8. Made a list of all persons we had harmed, and became willing to make amends to them all.
   9. Made direct amends to such people wherever possible, except when to do so would injure them or others.
   10. Continued to take personal inventory and when we were wrong promptly admitted it.
   11. Sought through prayer and meditation to improve our conscious contact with God as we understood Him, praying only for knowledge of His will for us and the power to carry that out.
   12. Having had a spiritual awakening as the result of these steps, we tried to carry this message to alcoholics and to practice these principles in all our affairs.

Alcoholics Anonymous: The Big Book, 4th Edition (New York: Alcoholics Anonymous World Services, 2002), p. 562.

2. "Weekend to Remember," Family Life Ministries http://www.familylife.com/weekend.

3. The Four Spirituals Laws were created in 1952 as a tract by Bill Bright used in the evangelical ministry Campus Crusade to win converts for Christ among students. Over the years, millions have been distributed.

4. *Mommy, Teach Me to Read!* (Nashville: B&H, 2007); *Mommy, Teach Me!* (Nashville: B&H, 2007); *The Mommy Survival Guide* (Kansas City: Beacon Hill, 2006); *Reaching the Left with the Right: Talking About Social Issues with People Who Don't Think Like You* (Kansas City: Beacon Hill, 2006); *Dirty Dancing at the Prom and Other Challenges Christian Teens Face: How Parents Can Help* (Kansas City: Beacon Hill, 2005); *The Mommy Manual: Planting Roots to Give Your Child Wings* (Ada, Mich.: Revell, 2005); *Lord, Please Meet Me In the Laundry Room: Heavenly Help for Earthly Moms* (Kansas City: Beacon Hill, 2004); *Ready Set Read! A Start-to-Finish Reading Program Any Parent Can Use* (Nashville: B&H, 1998); *Small Beginnings: First Steps to Prepare Your Toddler For Lifelong Learning* (Nashville: B&H, 1997).

5. Dr. R Albert Mohler, Jr., "Can Christians Use Birth Control?" June 5, 2012; http://www.albertmohler.com/2012/06/05/can-christians-use-birth-control-4/.

6. Quoted by Nicholas D. Kristof in "A Poverty Solution that Starts with a Hug," *New York Times*, January 7, 2012; http://www.nytimes.com/2012/01/08/opinion/sunday/kristof-a-poverty-solution-that-starts-with-a-hug.html.

7. Halah Touryalai, "Have $235,000? That's What It Takes to Raise a Child Today," *Forbes*, June 14, 2012; available at http://www.forbes.com/sites/halahtouryalai/2012/06/14/have-235000-thats-what-it-costs-to-raise-a-kid-today-before-college.

8. Rick Warren, *The Purpose Driven Life* (Grand Rapids: Zondervan, 2002).

9. Victor Hugo, *Les Miserables*, trans. Isabel F. Hapgood (New York: Thomas Y. Crowel, 1887), p. 105.

10. Peggy Noonan, "Culture of Death," *Wall Street Journal*, April 22, 1999; available at http://www.orthodoxytoday.org/articles2/NoonanCulture.php.

11. Nancy Helmich, "Parents Want to Be Teens' Pals," *USA Today*, October 12, 2004; available at http://www.usatoday.com/news/health/2004-10-12-parents-usat_x.htm.

12. Helmich, "Parents Want to Be Teens' Pals."

13. See http://www.terra.es/personal/asstib/articulos/perso/perso2.htm.

14. Catholic Education Research Center, "Television Statistics and Sources," available at http://catholiceducation.org/articles/parenting/pa0025.htm.

15. "TV Bloodbath: Violence on Prime Time Broadcast TV: A PTC State of the Television Industry Report," Parents Television Council, available at http://www.parentstv.org/ptc/publications/reports/stateindustryviolence/main.asp.

16. Carnegie-Mellon University, "Violence on Television: What do Children Learn? What Can Parents Do?" Available at http://www.cmu.edu/CSR/case_studies/tv_violence.html.

17. Jeffrey Johnson, et al. "Television viewing and aggressive behavior during adolescence and adulthood," *Science* 295, pp. 2468–2471 (2002).

18. Madigan, Tim. "TV Shows and Video Games Teach Children to Kill, Psychologist Says," *Fort Worth Star-Telegram*, May 10, 1999.

19. See http://www.parentstv.org/ptc/publications/reports/stateindustryviolence/main.asp.

20. Trednick, D.W., The Purpose of this Memorandum Is to Answer the Question "What Causes Smokers to Select Their First Brand of Cigarettes?"; available at http://legacy.library.ucsf.edu/tid/agv29d00.

21. See http://www.rand.org/pubs/research_briefs/RB9068/index1.html.
22. See Esther Entin, "Toddlers and TV: The American Academy of
    Pediatrics Says No," *The Atlantic*, available at http://www.theatlantic.
    com/health/archive/2011/10/toddlers-and-tv-the-american-
    academy-of-pediatrics-says-no/247402.
23. See Turn Off Your TV: "Kill Your Television," available at http://
    www.turnoffyourtv.com/ for resources and suggestions.
24. Quoted in Kurt Bruner, *The Divine Drama* (Wheaton, Ill.: Tyndale,
    2001), p. 13.
25. See "The Merchants of Cool," *Frontline*, PBS, available at http://
    www.pbs.org/wgbh/pages/frontline/shows/cool.
26. See http://www.statisticbrain.com/teenage-consumer-spending-
    statistics/; 2011 figures updated from Merchants of Cool figures:
    32 million teens/$100 billion spending power. If you missed "The
    Merchants of Cool," you can catch the complete fifty-three-minute
    show online at http://www.pbs.org/wgbh/pages/frontline/shows/
    cool, along with background interviews full of chilling insights into
    how the media and big corporations target our teens by encouraging
    and selling to the weakest parts of their character.
27. "Graduation Examination Questions of Saline County, Kansas,"
    Smokey Valley Genealogical Society and Library in Salina; available
    at http://www.rootsweb.ancestry.com/~kssvgs/school/exam1895/
    grad_exam.html.
28. See "Life expectancy in the USA, 1900-9," available at http://demog.
    berkeley.edu/~andrew/1918/figure2.html.
29. Ronald Reagan, "Farewell Speech to the Nation," January 11, 1989.
30. Bill Hendrick, "Benefits of Waiting for Sex Until Marriage,"
    WebMD, 28 December 2010; available at http://
    www.webmd.com/sex-relationships/news/20101227/
    theres-benefits-in-delaying-sex-until-marriage.
31. See http://usatoday30.usatoday.com/life/lifestyle/2004-09-06-teens-
    tv-sex-usat_x.htm.

32. Wendy Shalit, *A Return to Modesty: Discovering the Lost Virtue,* (New York: Touchstone, 2000).

33. Shalit, *A Return to Modesty,* p. 104.

34. See my article, "Is College for Everyone?" Available at http:// mommylife.net/archives/2010/04/is_college_for_2.html.

35. "American Idol Auditions Day 1 Maddy," YouTube video, viewable at http://youtu.be/fA_uUCFSPtQ.

36. Gary Chapman, *The 5 Love Languages: The Secret to Love That Lasts* (Chicago: Northfield, 2009).

37. Kahlil Gibran, *The Prophet* (Hertfordshire, U.K.: Wordsworth Editions, 1966), p. 14.

38. Quoted in Elyse M. Fitzpatrick and Jessica Thompson, *Give Them Grace: Dazzling Your Kids with the Love of Jesus* (Wheaton, Ill.: Crossway, 2011), p. 143.

39. Peggy Noonan, "Culture of Death," *The Wall Street Journal,* April 22, 1999; available at http://www.orthodoxytoday.org/articles2/ NoonanCulture.php.

ABOUT THE AUTHOR

Barbara Curtis, a convert to Catholicism in 2007, was a teacher, speaker, and the author of nine books. She has written for over sixty publications, including *Guideposts, Focus on the Family,* and *The Washington Post.* With her husband, Tripp, she helped raised twelve children (including three adopted sons with Down syndrome) and fourteen grandchildren.